PICTORIAL HISTORY
of
ARRAN

Andrew Boyle

Sarah and Bob

Thankyou for a lovely
Christmas

love Kate xxx

2001

Front cover
from an original painting
"ARRAN"
by Hugh Rankin

© Andrew Boyle

First Published in 1994
by Alloway Publishing Ltd.,
Darvel Ayrshire.

Printed in Scotland
by Walker & Connell Ltd.,
Hastings Square,
Darvel, Ayrshire.

ISBN No. 0-907526-57-8

PICTORIAL HISTORY
of
ARRAN

Andrew Boyle

Alloway Publishing

This book is dedicated to the beautiful

ISLE OF ARRAN

which has given so much pleasure to so many people.

All royalties derived from sales of the book are gifted to
THE ISLE OF ARRAN HERITAGE MUSEUM TRUST

INTRODUCTION

An island is a special place. Standing apart, it develops its own history and its own ethos. As an island of outstanding natural beauty with an interesting history, the Isle of Arran is as its Tourist Board claims — an island to treasure.

The lofty and serrated peaks of Arran rise from the sea and dominate the Firth of Clyde, adding grandeur to the world-famed waterway. When a flaming red sun is setting behind the island and bathing the sea in lustrous light, no words can express the splendour. In all seasons, Arran is a land that beckons and all who know it acknowledge that it has some indefinable quality that seduces you and calls you back.

My aim in compiling this book has not been to produce a learned account of Arran's history; the island's past, from antiquity to modern times, has been well researched and documented by many erudite authors whose works are readily available. I have omitted most of the heavier historical material, detail that discourages many people from taking an interest in history and which, in any case, would not be appropriate for this publication. I have tried to create an accurate, interesting and easily digested social history in which photographs form a commentary on the many facets of life on the island, past and present, complemented by a series of essays on similar themes.

So many things from the past have been all but forgotten, both their being and their meaning, even from no more distant than our parents' time. Mostly, they are simple things but in their time many were of more importance in the lives of our forebears than the major events of recorded history. With that in mind, I have concentrated on the ordinary things that affected, or still affect, the lives of ordinary people.

When writing on the history of a small community, it is difficult to avoid producing a mere rehash of what has gone before. Total originality is not possible but the pictorial format of this book is a new approach to the social history of the island and in the text some aspects of life on Arran in the past have been described more fully than has been done previously.

A work of this kind can not be compiled without the co-operation of many people and I have been very fortunate. I am indebted especially to four main sources of photographic material. Without access to the Isle of Arran Heritage Museum's archives, my task would have been almost impossible and I have to thank Mrs. Small, Mr. Finnie and Mrs. Gorman for the time they spent with my wife and I. For most of the modern photographs I required, I had to rely on Mr. Miller and his staff of the Arran Banner and they could not have been more helpful. The Arran Society of Glasgow, through Mr. McKelvie, allowed me to select from a collection of material which had been brought together for another purpose. Finally, Mrs. Margaret Stewart, Lamlash, was of great assistance with her interesting collection of Arran photographs.

My grateful thanks for their generous help are extended also to all of the people and organisations listed below:-

Mr. & Mrs. A. Blair, Rev. W.D. Lindsay, Mr. J. Rae, Mr. J. Bone, Mr. J. MacAlister, Mr. K. Robertson, Mr. J. Brown, Mrs. M. McArthur, Mr. I. Russell, Caledonian MacBrayne Ltd., Mr. W. McConnell, Mrs. P. Sillars, Mr. H. Cook, Mr. J. McGovern, Mr. I. Small, Mr. & Mrs. Chas. Currie, Mr. & Mrs. A. McHarg, Mr. & Mrs. D. Stewart, Mr. W. Dickie, Mr. I. McLean, The Potato Marketing Board, Mrs. M. Dickinson, Mr. J.F.M. MacLeod, The Scottish Farmer, Mr. Russell Duncan, Mr. H. McNicol, Mr. J. Thomas, Rev. D. Fulton, Mr. W. Marshall, Mr. E. Thorburn, Mr. R. Haddow, Mrs. C.C. Milne, Mrs. B. Turner, Mr. D. Johnson, Mr. G. Nicholson, Mr. & Mrs. H. Walker, Kilmory Kirk Session, Mr. G. Norris, Mrs. I. Walker, Mr. & Mrs. S. Lambie, Mrs. J. Pellow, Mr. K. Barnes, Mr. V. Small, Mr. E.C. Waugh, Mr. D. Robertson, Mr. & Mrs. D. Currie, Mrs. C. Kerr, Mr. G.B. Royffe.

When all of the material had been collected, a great deal of work remained to be done and it was made easier by being shared by my wife, Lilias, who helped with much of the research, selection of material, correction of the manuscript and proof reading.

A.B.

INDEX

A HISTORICAL SKETCH

In shape and substance, the Isle of Arran as we know it appeared first around 10,000 years ago, at the end of the last ice age. As it emerged bare and barren from an overlay of ice of great thickness, the island's glens had been gouged out by glaciers and its burns were carving channels to the sea. Arran's silhouette was as we see it with Goatfell as its highest point and the outline of a sleeping warrior recognisable in its ridges.

Born of volcanic might and majesty many aeons earlier, the land to be Arran had been changed time after time over millions of years as the stupendous forces of

Nature struggled towards stability in the wake of the earth's creation. At one period, the weight of ice up to a kilometre thick in places had pushed the land down into the earth's crust and allowed the sea to encroach but when the ice melted, the land rose again, evidence of which can be seen by the layman in the raised beaches that are still obvious around the island. The convulsions and convolutions of Arran's creation make it a mecca for students of geology. As expressed by Sir Archibald Geikie, President of the Royal Society, in Volume I of The Book of Arran, 'the island has a special claim to the admiration of all who take an interest in the ancient history of the globe.'

The time of man's arrival on Arran is not known. From sites on Machrie Moor and near Lochranza, there are indications of the presence of people over 8,000 years ago but they left us no readily discernible memorial of their existence. The earliest evidence of man that all can see are the chambered cairns of the Neolithic period (5000/6000 years ago) of which there are over twenty on the island. Of even more interest to those unversed in pre-history are the standing stones and circles of the Bronze Age (3000/4000 years ago); many of these monuments are well preserved and are a never-ending source of interest and perplexity to all who visit them.

On Arran, as elsewhere, it was Neolithic man who settled down and initiated the greatest revolution of all time; by cultivating land, sowing crops and domesticating animals, he began the science of agriculture and enabled the island to be inhabited and developed.

Christianity came to Arran no later than the 6th century, during which St. Molios spread the gospel on the island and used the cave on Holy Isle as a retreat. It is possible that earlier in the same century, Arran was visited by St. Brendan whose name, and probably his presence, have been commemorated in the naming of Kilbrannan Sound.

Over many centuries, Arran was merely a pawn on the geographical, political and cultural periphery of a field of play on which numerous forces struggled for supremacy in the making of Scotland. The influences of the Celts, Picts and Scots can be detected; the Vikings came as

The chambered cairn at Torrylin after it had been excavated in 1900. Human and animal bones were found in its four burial compartments.

PLATE III

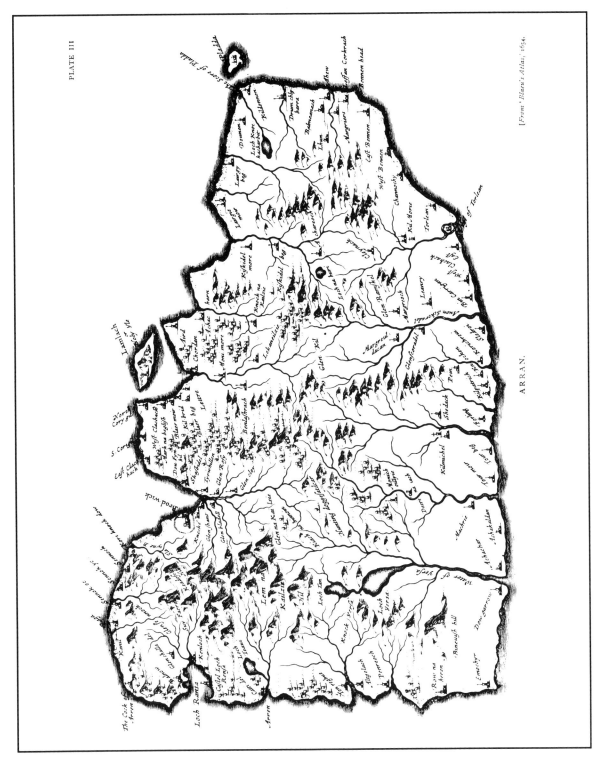

Blaeu's Map of Arran - 1654
The oldest map of the island.

Part of the raised beach north of Machrie.

raiders and stayed for 400 years; and the Lords of the Isles raided and colonized; all before the island finally became an integral part of Scotland in the 13th century.

Throughout the turmoil of change, the ordinary people of Arran would live out their lives, mentally and physically bent to the all-deflecting tasks required for survival, unconsciously absorbing or rejecting parts of the alien cultures to which they were subjected.

The people of the island would not be unaware of Scotland's 13th and 14th century Wars of Independence, but they had scarcely any involvement. One memorable exception was the brief sojourn by Robert Bruce as he girded his loins for the struggle to regain his Kingdom. It was from Kingscross that he set out in the early Spring of 1307, with his band of followers in 30 small boats, bound for his native Carrick and the long campaign that ended in England's recognition of Scotland as an independent nation.

For most of the 14th and 15th centuries, Arran was treated as a desirable piece of real estate to be bestowed by Royalty for favours or support. It passed through various hands - gifted, repossessed and gifted again, many times - before, in 1503, James Hamilton, son of Lord Hamilton, was created Earl of Arran by James IV, and granted all of the Royal lands on the island. Thus began what has been almost 500 years of unbroken ownership of, or other authority over, most of Arran by the Hamilton family.

The land granted to Hamilton did not include a part

owned by the Fullartons who had come to the island from Ayrshire in the 14th century, Lochranza Castle and much of the north-west corner of the island, which was owned by the Ayrshire Earl of Eglinton, or parts of the east and south-east belonging to the Stewarts of Bute. Over the

The coat of arms of the Fullartons of Kilmichael -
a crescent between three otters' heads, a camel head
and the motto 'Lux in tenebris'(light in darkness)

centuries that followed the Hamilton family spread their ownership to all but the land near Brodick owned by the Fullartons.

Few of Scotland's many tribulations of the 17th and 18th centuries had any appreciable effect on Arran, except for two occurrences which resulted from the 2nd Duke of Hamilton's support for the Royalist cause in the Civil War. In the first, the Covenanting Campbells of Argyll raided Arran in 1646, laid waste most of the island, destroyed homes and crops, and plundered animals and other property. The second occurrence was the occupation of Brodick Castle by Cromwellian troops in 1652, but it was an almost bloodless affair.

The imposition of stringent taxes after the Union of the Parliaments in 1707 was of great consequence to the island; it sparked off Arran's extensive involvement in the smuggling of contraband goods and the distillation of illicit whisky, all of which gave rise to many of the island's best-remembered legends. The illegal trade supplemented Arran's economy for almost 150 years but cost some of its people dearly in life and liberty. Life on the island had been wedded to the sea and for many men their seafaring skills stood them in good stead in smuggling, as it did in fishing and legitimate trading.

The Stuart rebellions of 1715 and 1745 barely touched the people of Arran. Of much greater import was the introduction in the last quarter of the 18th century of land-management schemes which resulted in the infamous Clearances. Hundreds of people were evicted from the land of their forebears to make way for new farming methods. Arran had been sorely neglected by its landowners and was far behind the development of Lowland Scotland. The mass of its people lived hard and comfortless lives in a hand-to-mouth existence and the loss of their homes and employment forced many families to move to the mainland or emigrate to North America.

Another great change of the period was in the language of the people. Gaelic was the native tongue but it was succumbing slowly to English. From early in the 18th century, reading and writing had been taught in English; this is attributed normally to outside pressures in favour of English but it was due equally to the dearth of text books in Gaelic. The people conversed in Gaelic but wrote in English. Gaelic was far from dead, however, and continued as the spoken language of the majority of islanders well into the second half of the 19th century.

The Clearances continued intermittently into the 19th century, which, in 1829, saw the largest single exodus of people from the island to the mainland or Canada, when a large number of families were cleared from the Sannox area to make way for deer and sheep. Although the sorrow and suffering of the dispossessed have sullied Arran's story, changes in the way of life on the island were both inevitable and overdue. As a consequence of the

Brodick Castle as sketched by Captain Francis Grose in 1772.
Grose was the man for whom Robert Burns wrote the poem "Tam O' Shanter"

Clearances, antiquated social systems were abandoned and larger land-holdings allowed vast improvements in agriculture.

The 19th century was a time of great advances in most aspects of life on Arran, due to steady improvements in the means of communication, internal and external. Paths over the muirs and round the coast-line, were made into roads suitable for, and allowing the introduction of, wheeled vehicles. Better connections with the mainland developed into regular and reliable services and improved all forms of trade to and from the island. Tourism, which had started slowly in the middle of the 18th century, increased steadily throughout the 19th, as the island became more accessible and holiday accommodation more available. As the island was developed, the living standards of its people improved.

During the 20th century, agriculture was joined and then surpassed by tourism as the mainstay of the island's economy. Whereas the number of people employed in agriculture has been greatly reduced by the introduction of new technology, the number employed in work related to the tourist trade has increased. In recent years, various commercial enterprises have been started, some of which have been very successful and have carried the name of Arran far and wide on the names of their products.

Arran has become a haven for the elderly and the owners of holiday homes, all of whom contribute to the island's economy and social life. However, most of the working life of the island goes on, independent of such contributions, and it is essential that adequate provision is made for a sufficient number of the younger generations to be able to live on Arran, as they are the island's life-blood. That must be the primary goal for the 21st and every succeeding century.

ANTIQUITIES & CASTLES

MACHRIE MOOR has one of Scotland's finest assemblages of ancient monuments, with stone circles, single stones, hut circles and burial cists all in one small area. The circle in the photograph is the best preserved of five on the moor. Dating from the Bronze Age (3000 to 4000 years ago), the circles were associated with burials and, as sacred places, were probably central to life in the ancient communities and held in awe for many centuries more.

Good minds have sought to unravel their secrets but they are still shrouded in mystery and the least imaginative visitor could not fail to be impressed by them. The finest stone circle on Arran is at Auchagallon, close to the coast road north of Machrie.

DRUMADOON POINT takes its name from the Iron Age doon (fort) which occupied about 12 acres of flat land on its summit. Unassailable from the shore due to the almost 100 feet high cliffs, the 2000 to 2500 years old doon was protected on the landward side by a dyke about 500 yards long, 10 feet thick and several feet high. Early chroniclers referred to the ruins of ancient dwellings, a standing stone and a spring of water within the doon. The size of the site indicates that when an attack was anticipated the doon would be a place of refuge for a whole tribe and their animals.

LOCHRANZA CASTLE is peculiarly located on a low spit of land jutting out into the loch. Little is known about its earliest history. The existing building dates from the 16th century but there had been a stronghold on the site as early as the 14th century. In 1400, reference was made to the 'Royal' castle of Lochranza. Although it was never of importance in the mainstream of Scottish history, it was raided, besieged and ravaged on several occasions, especially by the Lords of the Isles and their kinsmen. It was possessed in turn by John de Monteith, Campbells of Argyll, and one Ranald McAlister, before James II of Scotland granted it to Alexander Montgomerie, Lord Skelmorlie, in 1452. The Montgomeries retained it until 1705 when they handed it over, together with their Arran land, to Anne, Duchess of Hamilton, in payment of a debt. It is not known when occupancy of the castle ended and it was allowed to fall into disrepair.

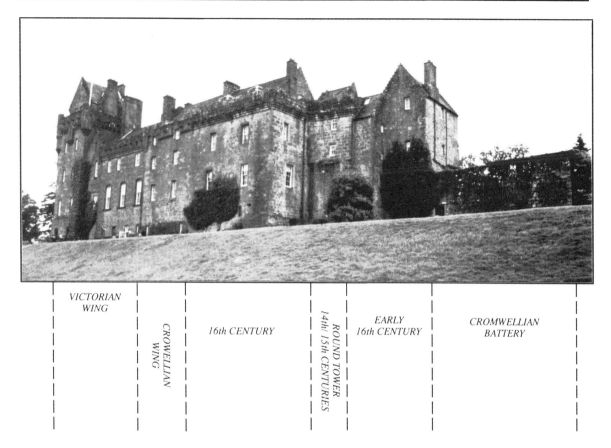

| VICTORIAN WING | CROMWELLIAN WING | 16th CENTURY | ROUND TOWER 14th/15th CENTURIES | EARLY 16th CENTURY | CROMWELLIAN BATTERY |

DEVELOPMENT OF BRODICK CASTLE

The oldest part of BRODICK CASTLE dates from the 13th century but fortifications stood on the site before that time. Well placed strategically in the Firth of Clyde, the castle has been garrisoned, raided and razed many times by competing forces.

In the 13th, 14th and 15th centuries, the fortress was garrisoned in turn by the troops of the Lords of the Isles, Edward I of England and the High Stewards of Scotland (later to be the Royal House of Stewart). In 1503, with most of Arran, it was granted by James IV of Scotland to James Hamilton, Earl of Arran, but its troubles were not over. In 1646, it was occupied by the Campbells of Argyll and in 1651 by Cromwellian troops, both occupations resulting from Hamilton support for the Royalist cause in the Civil War. During the latter occupation, a battery tower was added to the east end of the castle and a new wing to the west end. In 1660, the castle was returned to the Hamiltons but it was seldom used by the family until the 19th century. In 1844, a large extension was built onto the west end, producing the main entrance and imposing appearance we know today.

In 1957, on the death of the Dowager Duchess of Montrose (daughter of the 12th Duke of Hamilton), the castle and policies became the property of the Treasury in part-payment of death duties and they presented them to the National Trust for Scotland. In 1957, the Duchess's daughter, The Lady Jean Fforde, made a personal gift to the Trust of 7,300 acres of mountain and glen, including Goatfell, Cir Mhor, A'Chir and Glen Rosa.

The castle gardens are renowned for their rhododendrons. A door in the wall of the flower garden has the date 1710 but the flower and woodland gardens as we know them were created by the late Duchess of Montrose in the 1920's and 30's.

KILDONAN CASTLE occupies an impressive strategic position, overlooking the lower reaches of the Firth of Clyde, but it is not known to have played any important part in the history of Arran, far less of Scotland. It was a well-fortified four-storied tower, probably built in the 14th century. Almost nothing is known about its history except that in 1406 it was granted by King Robert III to his illegitimate son, John Stewart of Ardgowan, and that it was owned later by the Stewarts of Bute. It is in a ruinous and dangerous condition.

THE GIANTS' GRAVES, Whiting Bay, is, in fact, the remains of a late stone age burial chamber which, when constructed, would be covered by a large cairn of loose stones. Whereas the photograph was taken late in the 19th century, the structure is now engulfed by the forest. It can be reached by a well-signposted path which leads off the forestry road high above Whiting Bay, approached from Glen Ashdale.

THE SEA AND SHIPS

It is an odd feature of life on Arran at present that there is so little involvement with the sea. Although most of the people live close to the sea and are aware of it daily, for only a few is it part of their way of life; its many moods may be noted but only when the ferry is storm-bound or there is a threat from an exceptionally high tide, does the sea have any effect on daily life.

Things were not always so. The men of the island had a strong sea-faring tradition; they fished the waters around the island, served in the Royal or Merchant Navies, and pitted their wits and seamanship against the excisemen as smugglers.

At the beginning of the 19th century, several hundred young men left the island each year for naval service or to go deep-sea fishing from one of the large fishing ports. In the early years of this century, there was reckoned to be 29 Master Mariners in Lochranza and Catacol, and several more around the island. Even the generations of young men brought up on Arran as recently as the 1930's and 40's produced several Captains, Engineers and other seamen. Now, there are few who go to sea.

To reach the island, the first people to settle on Arran must have been familiar with boats and their skill would enable them to explore the coastline and trade with other settlements. Excavation of the earliest settlements on the island has shown that the ancient people ate shellfish, and it is likely that they fished the sea.

The Vikings settled on Arran for about 400 years and, as they integrated with the indigenous people, must have passed on their great sea-faring traditions. When King Hakon's mighty fleet of 120 vessels, many ornamented with the heads and necks of dragons, overlaid with gold, lay at anchor in Lamlash Bay in 1263, before the Battle of Largs, the islanders would have much more empathy with Hakon and his men than with King Alexander and his Scots who defeated them and ended Viking domination of the western islands.

That Arran was known for its fishing as early as the 15th century is shown by an entry in an account book of 1444, belonging to the household of King James IV, which records the purchase for the Royal Palace of a quantity of salted herring from the Isle of Arran. In 1695, reference was made to 'considerable fishing of cod and whiting in Lamlash Bay' and in 1776, a party of fishermen from Montrose settled in Lamlash and fished for cod, ling, haddock, whiting, flounders, and sole, some of which they sold at Saltcoats.

Most historians have asserted that on Arran commercial fishing was never more than a part-time occupation, confined to farmers and their workers fishing for herring in season. And yet, in 1845, Arran had 98 boats and 380 men employed in herring fishing, including 23 boats at Lamlash, 12 at Lochranza, 9 at Whiting Bay, 9 at Brodick, and 8 at Corrie, with the remainder spread around the island, mainly at Kildonan and on the west coast. It is difficult to accept that outwith the fourteen weeks or thereabouts of the herring season, all or even most of these boats, each a valuable asset to its owner, was laid up for the rest of the year while the men went back to work on the land. At a time when the sea 'teemed with fish', and work on the land was poorly paid, why would men turn their backs on the more lucrative occupation?

Although there were only 12 Lochranza boats fishing for herring

The trading smack 'Duchess' owned by Cook Brothers of Arran waiting to discharge her cargo at Kildonan in the 1880's

Lochranza Castle and Green

in 1845, the harbour was popular with herring boats from other areas. The Rev. Dr. David Landsborough, in his book 'Excursions in Arran', described what he saw in Lochranza in 1847: 'This is a place of rendezvous for the Highland boats during the herring-fishing season, and it is a lovely spectacle to see them launching forth in a summer evening, almost in countless numbers, covering the Sound of Kilbrandon (sic).' Later in the same passage he described the scene near Lochranza Castle when the boats returned: 'The green is strewed with fish and nets, and casks and carts, mingled with curers and coopers, and women and children.........boiling (fish) refuse that they may extract the oil.' Alas, within a few years the herring had deserted the area and the fishing declined almost to extinction.

By 1914, except for a few men fishing for herring out of Lochranza and Pirnmill, there was no fishing industry on Arran. In 1923, the trade had revived slightly and the island had 15 boats and 27 men employed. By 1933, the numbers were down to 4 boats and 10 men, and by 1955, 4 boats were after shell-fish only. Now, Arran's commercial fishing is confined to the part-time employment of a few men, mainly with lobster pots, while the waters around the island are fished by boats from Ayrshire and Kintyre.

Of all the lore relating to Arran, the greatest number of tales concern the daring sailors who turned to smuggling in the 18th and 19th centuries, at a time when the unlawful trade was close to being a national industry. The islanders were involved in two quite separate kinds of smuggling

operations, the first being the purchase and re-sale of contraband goods brought from foreign sources, and the second, the distilling and selling of illicit whisky, 'Arran Water' as it was known in Ayrshire.

In the first of these operations, Arran boats would rendezvous in the Firth with boats from France or the Isle of Man and purchase whatever contraband was on offer - probably French brandy or wine, Dutch gin, silks, tea, salt or tobacco. Under cover of darkness, often in tempestuous weather when the revenue cutters were less likely to be at sea, the contraband would be transported to a pre-arranged location on the Ayrshire coast where the cargo was re-sold for a handsome profit.

It was in the distillation and sale of the island's illicit whisky that Arran folk were most involved in smuggling. Substantial increases in the duty on spirits, together with restrictions on the amount of whisky legal distilleries were allowed to produce, caused a great increase in the price of legal whisky and resulted in a demand for illegally distilled whisky which, being free of duty, was very much cheaper. Illicit stills were operated all over Scotland and, around the Firth of Clyde no whisky was more popular than 'Arran Water'. James Paterson, an Ayrshire historian, described how, about 1820, as a young man in lodgings in Ayr, lodgings shared regularly with Arran sailors, he had wondered why kegs were kept under his bed until he found, inadvertently, that they were kegs of 'Arran Water'. He realised then that his landlady, who was renowned for the quality of the whisky she supplied to the gentry, even to the Sheriff of Ayr, was

The estate factor's yacht, nearest the camera, and the excisemen's cutter "Wickham" at Lamlash before 1886.

supplying them with illicit Arran whisky, unknown to the purchasers.

In 1784, Arran had 32 illegal stills, 23 of them at the south end of the island, and in spite of efforts to stop them, the number had increased to about 50 in 1797, with most of the whisky being transported off the island. The Duke of Hamilton threatened to dispossess any tenant convicted but as late as 1851 'Arran Water' was being seized by the Excise at Ayr harbour.

Both forms of smuggling were fraught with danger and several Arran people lost their lives or liberty. There are numerous true tales of conflict with the excisemen over almost 150 years. In 1711, a boat-owning Elder of Kilmory Parish kirk was suspended by the Session on suspicion of having smuggled tobacco onto Cumbrae. In 1754, three Arran men were banished to the plantations in America for life for assaulting an exciseman. In 1817, a boat loaded with illicit whisky had just left a beach at the south end of Arran when the crew saw a revenue cutter approaching. The smugglers turned back to the shore and were carrying their barrels up the beach when they were seized by the excisemen. A group of islanders who had gathered at the scene attacked the officers, whereupon the order was given for the excisemen to open fire, with the result that two men and a woman were shot dead and a boy and a girl injured. In 1822, three men set out from Brodick on a wild night, bound for Ayrshire with twelve casks of whisky, and all three were presumed drowned when their wrecked boat was washed ashore next morning between Ardrossan and Saltcoats.

During the same 150 years that Arran was involved in smuggling, the island, like all British coastal areas, was plagued by the Press Gangs. Conditions in the Royal Navy were so bad that few sailors would join the service voluntarily, so bands of armed sailors, each commanded by an officer, were sent out to abduct men and press them into the navy. They boarded merchantmen and seized most of each crew, and raided coastal towns and villages; either way, men who were caught were taken away for periods of service which were seldom less than five years. Most towns and villages on the coast had unofficial warning systems by which, when a raiding party was sighted or suspected an alarm was sounded and the men given time to escape into the countryside.

Arran's best Press Gang story relates to a local man called McCurdy, who was famed as an excellent seaman and daring smuggler. On one enterprise, he was intercepted by a revenue cutter but fought and defeated the excisemen. A reward of £500 was offered for his capture and, with great audacity, McCurdy gave himself up and claimed the money. He could have been tried and hanged or banished to the plantations but the Admiralty, desperate for sailors, had issued an instruction that when smugglers were caught they were to be pressed into the navy, so McCurdy was enlisted as a seaman on a man-of-war. Eventually, he was commissioned as an officer and rose to command a frigate. On patrol, his ship captured a French warship but after McCurdy had led a boarding party onto the vessel, the Frenchmen blew up their ship and McCurdy was killed in the explosion.

McCurdy's nephew, of the same name, joined the Royal Navy, whether by choice or abduction is not known, and by diligence rose to be Bosun of his ship. While engaged against the French in the Napoleonic Wars, he was sent out in charge of a party of men in a longboat, near the French coast. Under cover of a thick fog they were to reconnoitre and report on the dispositions of enemy warships in the area. They came unseen on a poorly guarded warship which they boarded and overcame the men on watch. Having done so, they battened down the hatches with the French crew below-decks, took possession of the ship and sailed it back to their own fleet. For his initiative, McCurdy was commissioned as an officer and later commanded a frigate, as his uncle had done. He retired to Arran and died in the 1850's.

Although small wooden boats, mainly smacks, were built at various places on Arran, the best remembered instance of boat building is the construction in 1894/5 of one of the earliest, possibly the first, of the small steam-powered cargo boats known as puffers. It was built of local wood in a field at Low Glencloy, by Adam Hamilton and his two sons, and was towed to Glasgow to have its engines fitted.

The puffers, later built of steel, gradually replaced the smacks and gabbarts as the 'pack horses' of west coast shipping, transporting coal, lime, cement, bricks, timber, etc. to the islands. Fifteen puffers were Arran owned: Roman; Kelpie; Glencloy (2); Invercloy (2); Glen Shira; River Cloy; Plover; Arran Rose; Arran Monarch; No. 10; Warlock; Airidhverga; and Ashdale Glen. Together with Spartan, Tuscan, Trojan and Cretan, the names invoke nostalgia in the generations who remember them.

A schedule prepared by Alister Kelso of Corrie in 1965, lists the vessels owned by Arran families between, roughly, 1850 and 1950. In all, 134 vessels are listed, of which 82 were smacks, 18 schooners, 15 puffers and 9 gabbarts. Seventeen of the vessels were lost at sea, many with all hands. A few Arran crews traded with foreign countries, mainly North America, and one vessel, at least, was trapped in North Atlantic pack-ice.

Many fine ships have weathered the storms of the world's oceans, only to come to grief in the shadow of the Sleeping Warrior. In their excellent book, 'Clyde Shipwrecks', Moir and Crawford give details of 72 vessels, large and small, which perished on or near the island between 1859 and 1955. From Dippen Head to the Sliddery Water is shown to have had 13 major shipwrecks, making it the most dangerous location in the Firth. The most dramatic was the loss of the wooden schooner 'Bessie Arnold' on 28th December, 1908. Some of the crew were drowned, four of whom are buried in Kilmory graveyard. Modern navigational aids have reduced the toll of the sea, nevertheless, the sinking of the fishing boat Antares by a submerged submarine off Sannox in 1990, with the loss of four lives, is a reminder that the sea is a treacherous environment.

Arran's seafaring traditions are upheld still by a few men and women, notably by the crew of the R.N.L.I. Inshore Rescue boat who are prepared to risk their lives to rescue others. A few men make a part-time living with lobster pots, while others take parties out on fishing trips

Launching of the Puffer "Glencloy" at Low Glencloy in 1895.

The vessels pictured at Lamlash old pier soon after 1884 are a topsail schooner, two trading smacks, the hulk of a schooner, and a steam yacht. The boat in the bay is a ketch.

or hire out small boats. Otherwise, for Arran, the sea is a place for pleasure sailing rather then employment.

One true story connects Arran men of the past and present. On a lonely South-Ayrshire shore near Lendalfoot, there is a little memorial: 'To Archibald Hamilton and his crew from Kingscross, Arran, who were drowned near this spot on 11th September, 1711.' A man from an old Arran family spent most of his working life in Ayrshire and drove past the memorial almost weekly. He did not know who or what it commemorated and always intended to stop and check. On his final journey before he was to retire and return to live on Arran, he stopped and read the inscription. Can you imagine his feelings when he saw that not only was it to the memory of Arran men but after

40 years of driving past, he had stopped on 11th September, 1990, exactly on the anniversary of the drowning.

The Lendalfoot memorial to Arran sailors

The Corrie smack, 'Betsy Crawford' unloading at Kildonan.

HOLY ISLE

HOLY ISLE derives its name from Mo'Laise - also called Molas, Molios and various other spellings - a Saint of the Celtic religion who lived on the island in the last quarter of the 6th century. Molaise was born in Ireland in 566 A.D. and arrived in Arran by way of Iona. The cave in which he lived is on the inner side of the island, about a mile south of the former farmhouse and twenty-five feet above high-water mark. Runic inscriptions in the cave show that it was used by Vikings, the earliest inscription dating from the 11th century and the latest from the time of the Battle of Largs in 1263.

Near the cave stands 'The Judgement Stone', which may have been used in religious ceremonies. It is an almost circular, flat topped rock with four seats cut out of the top edge; at the south side, steps lead up to the top, and a cross of curious shape has been cut into the east face. A few feet from the stone there is St. Molaise's Well, a spring to which healing powers have been attributed.

In the 13th century, a monastery was built on or near the site of the old farmhouse. It was already ruined in 1549 but its burial ground was in use until 1790.

In 1992, Holy Isle was bought by the Samye Ling Tibetan Buddhists who plan to build a monastery and two retreat centres, which will make the island once more a place of prayer and meditation

Lama Yeshe Losal the Retreat Master is pictured left.

Traditionally, bonfires were lit on the summit of Holy Isle to celebrate special events and that in the photograph was for Queen Victoria's Diamond Jubilee in 1897. In the forefront is the bearded John McIntyre, farmer on the Island in the second half of the 19th century, whose descendants still live in Lamlash.

ARRAN CURIOS

THE KING'S CAVE is just over a mile north of Drumadoon Point on the west coast of Arran. With the adjoining King's Larder and King's Stables caves, it is said to have been used by Robert Bruce, King Robert I of Scotland, and his followers, during their short stay on the island in 1307.

Early chroniclers associated the caves with the legendary Irish hero, Finn mac Cumhail, also called Fionn or Fingal, who is said to have visited Arran on hunting trips. The tradition connecting the caves with Bruce is fairly modern, nevertheless, they may have been used briefly by the King and his men when they landed on Arran from Rathlin Island. The King's Cave is claimed as the place where Bruce watched the persistent spider and was inspired to persevere in pursuit of his goal to rid Scotland of English domination. In fact, the attractive myth is probably no more than that and, although now traditional, is not ancient.

The King's Cave is up to 118 feet long, 44 feet wide and 50 feet high. At various parts the walls are decorated with ancient engravings from Pictish or early Christian times. Unfortunately, most of the engravings have been all but obliterated by vandalism.

During the 18th century, the King's Cave was used as a meeting place by Kilmory kirk session.

THE CAT STONE, a huge grey granite rock which sits on the landward edge of the road between Corrie and Sannox, features in one of Arran's best-known legends. The name Cat Stone is from the Gaelic clach a' chatha, 'stone of battle'.

Tradition maintains that hostility between the local population and Cromwellian troops occupying Brodick Castle in the 1650's culminated in a band of islanders attacking and killing all but one of a party of soldiers on patrol between Sannox and Corrie. The soldier who escaped sought refuge in the shelter of the Cat Stone but he was pursued, dragged from his hiding place and killed. Another version of the tale places it in Merkland Wood, near Brodick Castle.

The neatly drilled holes in the Cat Stone were made by an over enthusiastic Local Authority Roads Department employee who thought to improve the passage of traffic by blasting the rock. Fortunately, the intention became known to local residents before it was too late and after an acrimonious debate public opinion prevailed and the Cat Stone was saved.

ARRAN'S CURIOUS PILLAR-BOX, which stands at the side of The String, at its junction with Machrie Road, was built originally during the 1870's by David Wilson, a Shiskine stonemason. Col Currie of Shedog carried the mail and passengers between Brodick and Shiskine with a horse-drawn brake and a Dougarie Lodge servant was sent across Machrie Muir on horseback to collect or hand over the mail. A white-painted wooden post box was in use at the junction and when a horse shied at it and threw its rider, a new box was ordered and paid for by a guest at Dougarie Lodge. One tradition maintains that Wilson thought he had been paid too much money for his work and, to compensate, added the attractive carvings which are thought to be mason's tool-marks. During 1993 the pillar-box was demolished by a motor car, but was salvaged by Ian Stewart, Shiskine, and re-built by him in November, 1993.

John Watson Laurie

Edwin Rose

THE GOATFELL MURDER

On Friday, 12th July, 1889, Edwin Rose, a 32 years old London clerk and John Watson Laurie, a 25 years old Coatbridge pattern-maker (using the alias John Annandale), met on the paddle steamer Ivanhoe, sailing to Arran. They shared lodgings in Invercloy, Brodick, and on the afternoon of Monday, 15th July, set out to climb Goatfell. They were seen together on the summit about six o'clock but later in the day Laurie was alone in Corrie Hotel. He returned to his lodgings late that evening and early next morning left without paying his landlady, who thought both men had absconded. A few days later, Laurie was seen in Rothesay, wearing clothes identified later as having belonged to Rose. When Rose failed to return home, he was reported missing and after extensive searches on Arran his body was found on 4th August, concealed under a huge boulder on a slope of Coire nam Fuarnam. His face was 'terribly smashed' and his pockets had been rifled. After a nationwide search, Laurie was apprehended in Lanarkshire on 3rd September, claiming, "I robbed the man but I didn't murder him". After trial he was sentenced to death but two days before he was to hang, the sentence was commuted to life imprisonment and he spent the next 41 years in jail until he died in 1930. Edwin Rose was buried in Sannox graveyard with a granite boulder as his gravestone.

THE BESSIE ARNOLD FIGUREHEAD

On 28th December, 1908, in a blizzard, the three-masted wooden schooner Bessie Arnold, en route to Clydebank with a cargo of iron ore, ran aground on the rocky shore at Sliddery. Most of her crew were rescued by a rocket apparatus crew from Kildonan. Four men who died were buried in Kilmory kirkyard with the Bessie Arnold figurehead as their memorial. The figurehead has been refurbished by Mr. Thomas, Kilmory Manse, and removed from the kirkyard to prevent further deterioration. At time of writing, it is on display in the Isle of Arran Heritage Museum.

THE SAILOR'S GRAVE is situated on the landward side of an open grass area alongside the coast road, about half way between Lochranza and Catacol. The small memorial bears the inscription - 'John McLean, 12th August, 1854'. Tradition tells that McLean was a sailor who died of cholera on board his boat. He had made a shipmate promise to bury him on land but from fear of the disease the locals would not allow access to the graveyard. Under cover of darkness, the friend took the body ashore and buried it outwith the consecrated ground.

THE BAVARIAN SUMMER HOUSE in Brodick Castle's woodland garden was built in 1845 by the 10th Duke of Hamilton on the marriage of his son the Marquess of Douglas & Clydesdale to Princess Marie of Baden. The intrically patterned ceiling, created from fir cones of various shapes and sizes, is the original work of Bavarian craftsmen. The equally attractive interior wall panels were restored by the pupils of Priory Girls' School, Isle of Wight, from cones collected in the castle grounds.

THE DOCTOR'S BATH, CORRIE is on the foreshore at the south end of the village, about 50 yards south of Cromla House. Hewn out of the sandstone rock, between low and middle tide levels, the 'bath' is approximately 12 feet long, 5 feet wide and 5 feet deep, with steps cut out at one end. Early in the 19th century, Cromla was the home of a doctor McCredy and it was he who had the 'bath' created, possibly for some hydropathic treatment or, simply, to bathe in without the danger and discomfort of bathing from the rocky shore.

TOURISM

It was inevitable that tourists would come to Arran. A majestic and seemingly secluded place, as seen from afar, on the edge of Scotland's most populous area, was bound to attract attention and invite a visit. Of those who came, many came back, and back again, drawn by the island's beauty and some indefinable enchantment.

Holidaymakers first came to Arran at a time when most of its people were impoverished and their living conditions primitive. From the start, the holiday trade must have benefited a few of the islanders but it was almost 150 years before it was established as a major contributor to the island's economy. Now, the island's well-being depends on tourism.

The first known reference to Arran as a place to which to resort was made in 1746, the year in which Bonnie Prince Charlie was defeated at Culloden. In that year, it was recorded in the Ayr Burgh records that the town's Magistrates had changed the school holidays from May to June so that scholars could 'repair to Arran and other distant places for goat milk.' Drinking goat and ass milk was the health fad of the age. That the fad did not pass quickly is shown by an advertisement in The Glasgow Journal of 12th March, 1759: 'Good goat milk quarters may be had this season in the island of Arran, in a very commodious slated house hard by the castle of Brodick'. The advert went on to say: 'There is a packet boat settled to pass every week from Saltcoats to Arran for the convenience of travellers; the day she passes from Saltcoats is Thursday.'

In the 18th century, holiday visitors to Arran were

The 'slated house' at Cladach in 1993

almost exclusively of the upper classes; the working classes had neither the holidays nor the money to travel far from home. In a letter to Robert Burns, dated 22nd September, 1791, one of Ayrshire's gentry told the poet that her daughter had just returned from Arran, where she had spent the summer recuperating from illness. Obviously, the Arran air was already thought to be beneficial.

Although the island's popularity increased steadily, poor travel facilities hindered expansion of the holiday trade. The small sailing boats employed on the route could not give adequate service. Travellers wrote of waiting at Saltcoats for several days before a Captain was prepared to sail; others spoke of being becalmed at sea en route, whereby the crossing took several days and in one recorded case, the passengers and crew had to eat the produce one passenger was taking to market on the mainland, after they had exhausted other supplies during three days at sea.

As early as 1770, the Duke's Factor had realized that communications with the mainland had to be improved and called a meeting of leading citizens to 'take under consideration the establishment of a packet boat for service to this island.' The Factor's concern was for the establishing of trade links and was in no way connected with a desire to make the island more accessible for visitors. As it turned out, it was sixty years before there was any significant improvement in the service but when it did come it was dramatic.

During August, 1825, Arran had a preview of the improvement in store when the steam-powered S.S. Helensburgh paid visits to Lochranza, Lamlash and Brodick. Four years later, the island got its first regular steamer service when the Castle Company provided sailings from Glasgow to Brodick and Lamlash every

Tuesday and Saturday, with return sailings on Wednesdays and Mondays. The steamers proved immediately that they could provide a fast, reliable and cheap service and made Arran accessible for a greater number of people.

In 1834, the Castle Company was able to take advantage of Scotland's first passenger railway line between Troon and Kilmarnock by advertising a daily steamer service from Troon and Ardrossan to Brodick and Lamlash, complete with rail connections to and from Kilmarnock, making Arran the first Scottish island, and one of the earliest in the world, to have a rail and steamer service for visitors.

In the days of sail, Saltcoats was Ayrshire's main port of departure for Arran but with the advent of the steamers it was superseded by Ardrossan, with less frequent and mainly summer sailings from Troon and Ayr. At Ardrossan, the steamers connected with horse-drawn stage coaches from Glasgow and Kilmarnock but in spite of such restricted means of transport to the port, 7,000 passengers were conveyed to and from Arran during the summer of 1836.

A railway line was completed from Glasgow to Ardrossan in 1840 and from then the Glasgow and South Western Railway Company ran trains to connect with the Arran steamers at Ardrossan and the port secured almost all of the Arran trade. A steamer service between Glasgow and Arran continued into the 1860's but it operated only in summer and was patronized by passengers for whom speed was of no consequence.

During the 1850's and 60's, a daily service between Ardrossan and Arran was operated by the Ardrossan Steamboat Company but in 1868 the Company was unable to continue and the 12th Duke of Hamilton took over the running of the service. The Duke's enterprise proved to be a failure and in 1874 Captain William Buchanan, a prominent operator on the upper reaches of the Firth was asked to take over the run. The Buchanan steamers provided a good service all year round to Corrie, Brodick, Lamlash, Kingscross and Whiting Bay, which was supplemented by other operators each summer, and encouraged by the excellent service, the number of visitors increased steadily.

The Campbeltown and Glasgow Steam Packet Company operated a daily service which called at

Lochranza and Pirnmill but it was inadequate and unreliable. Another operator started a service from Fairlie to Lochranza and Campbeltown but it was equally unreliable and lasted for only a few years. The poor service to the villages on the west coast of Arran deprived them of the full benefits of the holiday trade until angry public meetings in Lochranza and Pirnmill in 1895 demanded and got improvements.

The greatest handicap to the growth of tourism on Arran was the lack of piers. At every village where steamers called, passengers disembarking had to be transferred into small boats and rowed ashore. Naturally, the inconvenience and well-proven danger of the transfer kept many people from visiting the island. The first pier was built at Brodick in 1872, followed by Lamlash in 1884, Lochranza in 1889 and Whiting Bay in 1901. Until the 1930's, steamers still called regularly at Corrie, Kingscross and Pirnmill, and occasionally at Machrie, Blackwaterfoot and Kildonan, at each of which no suitable pier was ever built.

The next significant improvement in Arran's accessibility was in 1890. The Glasgow and South Western Railway Company, while conveying passengers by rail from Glasgow to Ardrossan, had not entered the steamer trade, preferring to leave the service with the Buchanan family, however, their railway rivals, the Caledonian Railway Company opened a new line from Glasgow to Ardrossan and put a steamer on the Arran run in direct competition with the Buchanans. To ensure success, the Caledonian Company operated a new train, the Arran Express, and a new steamer, the Duchess of Hamilton, the fastest boat on the Clyde until that time.

The competition on the Arran run led to many exciting scenes which caught the public's imagination and gave the island a lot of free publicity. At times, common sense and caution were neglected and lives endangered. On 1st July, 1890, because Buchanan's Scotia was due to leave three minutes later, the Duchess of Hamilton moved away from Brodick pier while people were embarking, leaving some on the gangway, suspended over the water. A few months later, the Duchess left Brodick ten minutes after the Scotia and gradually overhauled it on the voyage. The vessels were neck and neck as they approached Ardrossan harbour and neither Captain would give way as they passed through the narrow entrance at the breakwater, whereby the steamers collided and almost struck a third inside the harbour. The Captain of the Duchess was fined but racing continued for many years.

The Buchanan boats could not match the speed of the Duchess of Hamilton and in the 1890/91 season both the Buchanans and the G. & S.W.R. lost three-quarters of their trade to the Caledonian Company. The losers had to respond or surrender the route and in 1892 the G. & S.W.R. took over the Buchanan service with a new boat, the Glen Sannox, which was faster even than the Duchess.

It was during this period of fierce competition that the fastest journey times between Glasgow and Arran were set, times which have never been improved. When she was introduced, the Duchess of Hamilton reduced the time to ninety minutes, achieved by dispatching a separate train with the luggage from Glasgow to Ardrossan a few minutes ahead of the boat train, so that the luggage could be transferred without delaying the Duchess. From its start in 1892, the Glen Sannox reduced the time to eighty minutes, due mainly to the vessels' speed on the crossing. Such fast journey times allowed Arran to compete more

REGULAR COMMUNICATION BY STEAM
BETWEEN

THE AYRSHIRE COAST
AND

ISLAND OF ARRAN.

FOR the accommodation of Parties in the Neighbourhood of KILMARNOCK, IRVINE, KILWINNING, SALTCOATS, TROON, and ARDROSSAN—

THE GLASGOW CASTLES STEAM-PACKET COMPANY continues to Run one of their Packets regularly (Weather permitting) between TROON, ARDROSSAN, BRODICK and LAMLASH,—Leaving TROON at Half-past 8, and ARDROSSAN at 10 o'Clock Morning; and will Return to Troon in the Afternoon, by the same route, leaving BRODICK at 5 o'Clock.

Arrangements have been made with the Proprietors of the RAILWAY CARRIAGES to convey Passengers from KILMARNOCK, &c., to TROON, in time for the Packet's Sailing, and to await her Return in the Evening.

By the above arrangement, Parties from the Ayrshire Coast will have an excellent opportunity of visiting, at a trifling expense, the beautiful and romantic Scenery of the ISLE of ARRAN—and, after remaining there nearly Six Hours, can return to their own homes in the Evening.

At the request of numerous Parties visiting Troon and Ardrossan, the Castle Company intend, during the Summer Months, to allot One Day in each Week, (Wednesdays) for the express purpose of going on Pleasure Excursions, when an opportunity will be thus afforded of visiting most of the celebrated and beautiful places in the Frith of Clyde.

☞ From and after TUESDAY, the 26th August, the INVERARY CASTLE will (until further notice) continue to Ply, every Lawful Day, between Troon, Ardrossan and Brodick, and Lamlash—returning in the Evening.

JOHN ANDERSON, Manager.

CASTLES STEAM-PACKET OFFICE,
Glasgow, August 25, 1834.

An 1843 Advert re the P.S. Inverary Castle

TO ISLAND OF ARRAN,
Via ARDROSSAN.

Commencing TO-DAY (SATURDAY), 31st Current, the Caledonian Company will Run an EXPRESS SERVICE OF TRAINS between GLASGOW (Central Station) and ARDROSSAN, in connection with the New Saloon Steamer DUCHESS OF HAMILTON, to and from ARRAN, the Journey being accomplished in 90 minutes.
The Train and Steamboat Service will be as under :—

GLASGOW TO ARDROSSAN.

	A.		B.	
	A.M.	P.M.	P.M.	P.M.
Glasgow (Central Station), Dep..	8.45	1.45	4.45	5.13
„ (Eglinton St. Station), „	8.49	1.49	4.49	5.16
Ardrossan Station........Arrive	9.34	2.28	—	6.10
„ Pier	9.35	2.30	5.30	6.12
„ Pier ....Depart	9.40	2.35	5.35	6.20
Brodick ....Arrive	10.20	3.15	6.15	7 0
Lamlash .... „	10.40	3.35	6.35	7.20
Whiting Bay .... „	11.0	3.55	6.55	7.40

ARDROSSAN TO GLASGOW.

	C.	D.			A.
	A.M.	A.M.	P.M.	P.M.	P.M.
Whiting Bay ..Depart	6.50	7.5	12.30	3.15	4.15
Lamlash ...... „	7.10	7.25	12.50	3.35	4.35
Brodick ...... „	7.30	7.45	1.10	3.55	4.55
Ardrossan Pier..Arrive	8.10	8 25	1.50	4.75	5.35
Ardrossan Pier..Depart	8.15	8.30	1.55	4.40	5.40
„ Station „	—	—	2.0	4.33	5 45
Glas.(Eglin.St.Sta.)D'p	8.56	9.12	2.59	5.35	6.31
„ (Central Sta'n.)Arr.	9.0	9.15	3.3	5.40	6.35

A. Saturdays only.   C. Mondays only.
B. Daily except Saturdays. D. Daily except Mondays.

DAILY EXCURSIONS are made (Saturday excepted) from ARDROSSAN and the ARRAN PORTS to AILSA CRAIG, ROUND ARRAN, ROUND BUTE, or to CAMPBELTOWN, from Ardrossan on arrival of the 8.45 A.M. Train from Glasgow (Central Station).

RETURN FARES—

	1st Class and Steamer.	3d Class and Steamer.
Glasgow and Arran........	5s 6d	3s 9d
Do. Excursion....	7s	
Ardrossan and Arran........Cabin, 2s.		Steerage, 1s 6d.
Do. Excursion.... „ 3s.		„ 2s.
Arran and Do. „ 2s.		„ 1s 6d.

The Trip on MONDAY, 2d June, will be ROUND AILSA CRAIG, and on TUESDAY ROUND ARRAN. WEDNESDAY to CAMPBELTOWN.

CIRCULAR TOUR Daily going via GOUROCK or WEMYSS BAY and returning via ARDROSSAN or vice versa.

Caledonian Steam Packet Co., Limited,
302 Buchanan Street, Glasgow.

An 1890 advert re the P.S. Duchess of Hamilton

and operated steamers under the name, Caledonian Steam Packet Company and after further changes formed the basis of the present operators, Caledonian MacBrayne. The quality of the ferry service has always had a bearing on the success of tourism on Arran and, in spite of regular criticism, 'Cal Mac' have not failed the island.

Throughout the 19th century, Arran's holidaymakers were mainly still of the upper classes. Most wealthy families who holidayed on the island took the let of a large villa for several weeks or months in summer and arrived complete with servants. In 1893, the G. & S.W.R. advertised a special sailing from Ardrossan to Corrie, Brodick, Lamlash and Whiting Bay - 'for the convenience of families removing to Arran.'

Hotel accommodation of a reasonable standard was scarce for most of the 19th century. There were several inns around the island, some of which were referred to by visitors. In 1840, the inn at Urinbeg, Lochranza, was patronized and praised by the Rev. Dr. David Landsborough, Minister of Stevenston and writer on Arran; a visitor to Lamlash Fair in 1876, wrote disparagingly of the village inns being 'redolent of whisky and whisky songs'; and as referred to earlier, the two-storey house at Cladach was advertised in 1759 as 'good goat milk quarters.' Lagg Hotel is probably the oldest hotel on the island, dating from about 1791, followed closely by Kildonan Hotel from about 1800. Douglas Hotel, Brodick was started in 1856. In 1876, a visitor who left Brodick on foot at daybreak on a summer morning, called at 'Ranza Inn' about nine o'clock to be told that breakfast would not be ready for an hour; he called back an hour later and found the dining-room full, which suggests that even then Lochranza was popular with visitors.

The Dukes of Hamilton restricted development of Arran for most of the 19th century, much to the displeasure of many local people. In the New Statistical Account, of 1840, the Lamlash Minister suggested that if the restrictions were lifted - 'opulent individuals from Glasgow and Ayrshire would in a few years ornament the whole line of coast from Sannox to Largiebeg with a succession of neat summer habitations for themselves and families, and make Arran the most attractive island in the West Highlands.' Few people, residents or visitors, will be other than delighted that the

favourably with the resorts on the upper reaches of the Firth.

In 1923, the rival railway companies amalgamated

The Boathouse, Brodick, as sketched in 1874

Minister's vision has not come to pass. In 1856, Douglas Row and Alma Terrace, both in Brodick, were built to house families displaced from near the castle but the tenants were not allowed to accommodate holidaymakers. Many of the island's hotels and large villas were built in the last few years of the century.

Accommodation for less affluent visitors was far from satisfactory, even late in the 19th century. Most of them lodged in cottages, many of which lacked basic comforts. In 1877, a visitor found lodgings in a dwelling called The Boathouse which stood at the foot of Fisherman's Road (opposite Brodick school). He described the house as being an upturned boat on walls two or three feet high, divided internally into a but and ben, each with a box bed. Joined to the main building were several outhouses, some with upturned boats for roofs, each being a lodging with a bed, a small table and a washbasin. Breakfast at dawn was his own bread and butter, washed down with spring water. A giant snail had buried its head and horns in his butter, a family of mice were at home in his room, and a hen and chicks wandered in if he left his door open.

Tourism on Arran reached its peak shortly before the First World War. It declined throughout the depression of the 1920's but revived in the 30's. The duration of the Second World War and into the 1950's was another boom period, rivalling any that had gone before, but it was followed by many lean years. Lamlash and Whiting Bay lost their piers in 1954 and 1957 respectively, and both villages were badly effected for several years. Lochranza pier, although never officially closed, went out of use in 1957 and was finally swept away in a storm in 1989.

Fortunately for Lochranza, the summer service from the slipway to Claonaig brings extra tourists to the village.

As the popularity of foreign holidays increased, Arran's trade suffered but now it shows signs of recovery. The smaller villages had never had the high volume of visitors known by Lamlash, Brodick or Whiting Bay, and many of their holiday families stayed loyal to them through the lean years.

An important part of the island's holiday trade has always been the letting of private houses and this business has never been as badly hit during recessionary periods as the hotels and boarding houses. Many families on Arran have a small 'back' house which they move into for the summer months while they let their main residence, or vice versa. The hotel and boarding house trade has declined dramatically in recent years and many of the

Captain William Buchanan, succeeded by his sons, operated Clyde Steamers for about 75 years, owning the largest fleet for many years. He built Kinneil House, Lamlash in 1885 and was the only fleet owner to live on the island

Lagg Hotel in 1903

properties have been converted into holiday flats which are now very popular.

The greatest change in the island's tourist trade in modern times came with the introduction in 1957 of the car ferry Glen Sannox. Since then, succeeding ferries have had steadily increasing vehicle capacities, resulting in an ever increasing influx of cars to the island. The great volume of cars is said by many people to have spoiled the character of the island but for those who are able to leave the macadamized roads, more than 90% of Arran is still unspoiled. The many advantages of visitors' cars should not be overlooked; they have given the smaller villages a much larger share of the benefits of tourism as visitors have explored the island, and many families are happy to holiday in places they would have considered too remote without a car.

There is nothing in Arran's economy as important as tourism. Fortunately, the considerable effort required to at least maintain and hopefully improve the island's trade is expended and co-ordinated in a thoroughly professional manner by the Isle of Arran Tourist Board. Through their Projects Officer, his deputy, and a small staff, the Board work hard to promote the island as a holiday resort, to provide a service to visitors, and to improve the standards of accommodation and amenities.

The Pirnmill Ferry in 1890

THE PRINCIPAL VESSELS ON THE ARRAN SERVICES SINCE 1834

Type	Built	Name	Period (approx.)	Owner

ARDROSSAN - ARRAN

Type	Built	Name	Period (approx.)	Owner
PS	1820	Inverary Castle	1834-39	Castle Company
PS	1847	Isle of Arran	1847-60	Ardrossan Steamboat Coy.
PS	1860	Earl of Arran	1860-68	Ardrossan Steamboat Coy.
PS	1868	The Lady Mary	1868-71	Duke of Hamilton
PS	1871	Heather Bell	1871-74	Duke of Hamilton
PS	1865	Rothesay Castle	1874-78	Captain Buchanan
PS	1878	Brodick Castle	1878-87	Captain Buchanan
PS	1880	Scotia	1887-92	Captain Buchanan
PS	1890	Duchess of Hamilton	1890-1906	Caledonian Steam Packet Co.
PS	1891	Marchioness of Lorne	1891-1914	Caledonian Steam Packet Co.
PS	1892	Glen Sannox	1892-1925	Glasgow & South Western Railway
PS	1893	Glen Rosa	1893-1939	Glasgow & South Western Railway
TSS	1906	Duchess of Argyll	1919-36	Caledonian Steam Packet Co.
TSS	1906	Atlanta	1906-37	Glasgow & South Western Railway
TSS	1925	Glen Sannox	1925-36	London Midland & Scottish Railway
TSS	1936	Marchioness of Graham	1936-57	Caledonian Steam Packet Co.
MV	1957	Glen Sannox	1957-70	Caledonian Steam Packet Co.
MV	1966	Caledonia	1970-82	Caledonian Steam Packet Co.
MV	1964	Clansman	1982-84	Caledonian MacBrayne Ltd.
MV	1984	Isle of Arran	1984-93	Caledonian MacBrayne Ltd.
MV	1993	Caledonian Isles	1993-	Caledonian MacBrayne Ltd.

GLASGOW/GREENOCK/FAIRLIE - LOCHRANZA/PIRNMILL/CAMPBELTOWN

Type	Built	Name	Period (approx.)	Owner
PS	1848	Celt	1848-67	Campbeltown & Glasgow Steam Packet Co.
PS	1853	Druid	1853-68	Campbeltown & Glasgow Steam Packet Co.
PS	1866	Argyll	1885-90	Various
PS	1867	Gael	1867-85	Campbeltown & Glasgow Steam Packet Co.
SS	1868	Kintyre	1868-1907	Campbeltown & Glasgow Steam Packet Co.
SS	1878	Kinloch	1878-1926	Campbeltown & Glasgow Steam Packet Co.
SS	1885	Davaar	1885-1939	Campbeltown & Glasgow Steam Packet Co.
PS	1886	Victoria	1890-93	Various
TSS	1901	King Edward	1901-52	Turbine Steamers Ltd.
TSS	1902	Queen Alexandria	1902-12	Turbine Steamers Ltd.
TSS	1912	Queen Alexandria	1912-35	Turbine Steamers Ltd.
TSS	1926	Dalriada	1926-40	Turbine Steamers Ltd.
TSS	1932	Duchess of Hamilton	1946-70	Caledonian Steam Packet Co.

GLASGOW - ARRAN (various piers)

Type	Built	Name	Period (approx.)	Owner
PS	1869	Guinevere	1869-85	Various
PS	1877	Glen Rosa	1877-81	Shearer Brothers
PS	1880	Ivanhoe	1880-97	Various
PS	1895	Duchess of Rothesay	1895-1946	Firth of Clyde Steamers
PS	1896	Jupiter	1896-1935	Glasgow & South Western Railway

LOCHRANZA - CLONAIG

Type	Built	Name	Period (approx.)	Owner
MV	1972	Kilbrannan	1972-73	Caledonian MacBrayne Ltd.
MV	1973	Rhum	1973-87	Caledonian MacBrayne Ltd.
MV	1987	Lochranza	1987-92	Caledonian MacBrayne Ltd.
MV	1992	Loch Tarbert	1992-	Caledonian MacBrayne Ltd.

PS - Paddle Steamer   TSS - Twin Screw Steamer   SS - Screw Steamer   MV - Motor Vessel

P.S. Duchess of Hamilton (1890)

P.S. Glen Sannox (1892)

T.S.S. Marchioness of Graham (1936)

M.V. Glen Sannox (1957)

SCHOOLS

ARRAN HIGH SCHOOL building was completed in 1941 but taken over immediately as a naval barracks for the duration of the war. In 1946, it opened as Lamlash Secondary School enabling pupils from all over Arran to come together for their secondary education for the first time. Pupils who wanted to continue beyond leaving age still had to do so at Rothesay Academy or various schools on the mainland. In 1962, the name was changed to Arran High School and in 1974 the school was upgraded from a 4-year to a 6-year Secondary, ending the need for schooling to be completed off the island.

Whereas, in 1957, the school had a pupil capacity of 300, with 240 on the roll, and was staffed by a Headmaster and 10 Secondary teachers, 35 years later the figures had increased to a capacity of 384, with 305 on the roll, and staffed by a Headmaster and 29 teachers (full and part-time). Increasing numbers has necessitated several extensions to the original building and now it is more than twice its original size.

There are primary schools in Brodick, Corrie, Pirnmill, Shiskine, Kilmory, Whiting Bay and Lamlash, the last-named being adjacent to Arran High School.

A CLASS OF 1946/47

One of the first classes in the new school comprised of young people from Brodick, Lamlash, Whiting Bay, Kilmory and Shiskine. Back row: J. B. Petrie (Headmaster); Duncan Dewar; Hugh Leitch; Stewart Currie; Robert Hamilton; Stewart Lambie; Jack Lang; John Corbett; Miss McInnes (Teacher). Front row: Margaret Rierie; Jenny Crawford; Mhairi McDowall; Margaret Bannatyne; May Johnstone; Georgina McSkimming; Irma Bowden; Sadie Girvan; Susan Irvine.

LOCHRANZA SCHOOL - 1906

This photograph of the staff and pupils of Lochranza School in 1906 includes children from Lochranza, Catacol, Cock and Newton. Most of the family names are still common in the villages.

Front row: Tom Kerr; Ronald McAlister; Gilbert Kerr; Jimmy Gillan; Jackie Gillan; Innes McMillan; George McAlpine; Miller Cran; Nigel Kerr.

Second row: Nancy Brid; Janet Clark; Cissie Gillan; Betty Kerr; John Clark; Bob Wilson; Charlie Bridgend; Mary Kerr; Mary McAlpine; Cathy McAlister; Jessie Kerr.

Third Row: Mr. Archie McAlister; Duncan Kerr; John Kerr; Robert Kerr; Jimmie Kerr; Grant McAlister; Bel McKie; Miss Campbell.

Fourth row: Bobby Kerr; Baldy McMillan; Tom Gillan; Dougal Kerr; Bell McKie; Mary Kerr.

Back row: Mary Kerr; Flora McCosko; Flora McMillan; Betty Bridgend; Janet McAlister; Dina McMillan; Marion Murchie; Mary Bridgend; Annie Hendry.

THE CLEARANCES

The Clearances are the part of Arran's history referred to most often by the people of the island. The name, Clearances, may be too emotive, too significant in the minds of Scottish people, to describe properly what took place on the island. Arran saw none of the ruthless and barbaric treatment of people such as has stained the name of the 2nd Duke of Sutherland for almost 200 years.

It may be said that the difference between the Arran Clearances and those in other parts of the highlands and islands was only one of degree; in reality, the difference was so great that comparison is barely appropriate. For example, whereas on Arran over about 60 years, probably no more than 150 families were dispossessed of their land and livelihood, in Sutherland alone 15,000 people were evicted between 1811 and 1820, including 1,000 from one glen in one day. On Arran, no physical force was used in evictions; in Sutherland, and other places, families were burned out of their homes and left to face winter weather without food, shelter or employment.

It can not be doubted that in the 18th century

A sketch of an Arran blackhouse

improvements were overdue on Arran, improvements in living conditions, diet, farming methods, rights of tenure, diversity of employment, and lots more. Living standards were miserably low and the people were trapped in the bondage of unremitting labour required to exist. In many aspects of life, the island was at least fifty years behind the standards of Lowland Scotland. As late as the 1840's, a visitor observed about some of the houses on the island that they were the poorest cottages he had ever seen inhabited by human beings. However, before judgement is passed on the rights and wrongs of the Arran Clearances, it is necessary to know more about the conditions in which people lived.

The majority of Arran people lived in large clachans which were groups of dwellings, each with a few outbuildings. Families lived in low cottages, the walls of which were built of loose stones stopped with turf and clay; the roofs were thatched with heather or straw, held down by a network of heather ropes weighted with large stones. Inside, the best of the cottages were divided by light partition walls into three compartments, a byre for the cattle and two rooms - a but and a ben - for the family. There were two doors from outside, one to the byre and one to the dwelling. The dwelling door led into the 'but', from which inner doors gave access to the byre and to the 'ben'. The 'but' had an open hearth in the middle of an earthen floor; smoke from the fire was supposed to escape through a hole in the roof but most of it stayed in the room, blackening the interior; the 'but' window had only a rough wooden shutter to keep out the elements. The 'ben' or inner room was where the family gathered; it had a stone-built fireplace with a proper chimney, one glazed window and a wooden floor. Two narrow box beds were built into the wall between the 'but' and 'ben'; the rest of

the family slept in the roof space under the thatch, even above the byre if necessary. There was no sanitation, no drainage system and no running water. The families of cottars (labourers) could not aspire to even the standard of dwelling described. Most of their cottages were smaller and had only one room with an earthen floor, no glazed window, and an open fire without a chimney.

For the common people, the diet was monotonous, based on oatmeal (as porridge, brose and bannocks); barley (as soup or flour); potatoes; a little cheese; and salt herring. Bread was oatcakes or bannocks, and meat, regarded as an occasional luxury, was dried goat flesh or braxy mutton (the flesh of a sheep that had died of brain disease or accident). In winter, when food was scarce, cattle were bled and the blood mixed with oatmeal to make a dish similar to our black pudding.

All but a few people depended on the land for their living. The families of the clachans worked communally, although they had rights to pieces of land individually. Allocation and cultivation of land was by the ancient and inefficient celtic system called runrig, which has been described in the section on agriculture.

It is difficult to know how people grew enough food to survive. Fourteen families lived around the Cock and Laggan; over 100 adults and children lived in North Glen Sannox; at least 12 families lived in Glen Catacol; Shannochie had 15 families; and there were between 10 and 15 families at each of Gargadale, Thundergay and Blairbeg. At all of these examples, the acreage of good land was small and even with modern methods, implements and fertilizers, it would be impossible to make a reasonable living for more than a few folk.

Such then were the circumstances of life and work for

Laggantuine, near the Cock of Arran. Although generally said to be 'Clearances' ruins the dwellings may have been abandoned due to a 19th century outbreak of plague.

ordinary people on Arran in the 18th and early 19th centuries. Things had to change and the people must have known it. They may have been less well educated than ordinary people are at present but they were no less intelligent. We do them no justice if we doubt that they would have wished for a better way of life for themselves and their families.

In 1766, the Duke of Hamilton's Trustees invited John Burrel, Factor for another of the Hamilton estates, to visit Arran and make recommendations for re-organising land management on the island. To the Trustees, better land use meant a means of obtaining a greater income from rents. Burrel's plans were designed, above all else, towards the abolition of the runrig system and the communal holding of land. Most of the leases were due for renewal in 1772 and by then Burrel was ready to implement his changes. When leases came up for renewal they were refused and that was the start of the Arran Clearances which were to last on and off for the next 70 years or more.

It is not necessary to give the details of Burrel's plans or their consequences. Suffice to say that leases which had been refused were grouped into larger holdings and most families were left without land. Men had to seek employment with the neighbour who had been favoured with one of the large holdings and if not successful had to look for both new work and new homes.

From that time on, families who had been dispossessed began to leave the island, some finding work in farming on the mainland or in the new industries in the towns and cities. Other families emigrated, mainly to North America. Those who chose to stay on the island moved to the coastal settlements, where they built new hovels for themselves and the men took up work as fishermen or in the production of kelp, or both.

Full implementation of Burrel's plans were frustrated by the people at every opportunity and, on occasion, by the Duke's reluctance to evict too many families while there was not a reasonable amount of alternative employment on the island. Burrel planned a greater diversity of work but the small projects he introduced, even if they had thrived, would have been totally inadequate to provide for the number of men left without a means of making a livelihood. He encouraged fishing, kelp production, and a variety of small crafts; slate was quarried at Lochranza, limestone quarried at Corrie, and coal dug at the Cock, but the operations were either unsuccessful or employed few men.

John Burrel's connection with Arran ended in 1782. In the 16 years since his first visit to the island, he had become possibly the most hated man in its modern history. His plans were far from being fully implemented but he had torn asunder a way of life which had existed for centuries and in doing so had dispossessed hundreds of people of all but life itself. Oddly, although he was only the Duke's agent and could not act without authority, most of the hatred was directed at the Factor and not the Duke.

Displacement of families and a measure of emigration continued but by comparison with what had gone before,

*The 18th century runrig farms and coastal settlements
in North Arran.*

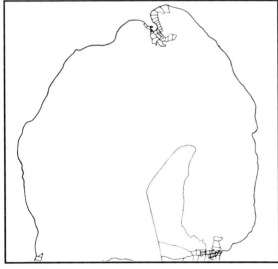

*The 1814 plan to clear North Arran of settlements to
make way for deer and sheep*

the island had a period of stability after Burrel's departure. The coastal settlements benefited from an improvement in the kelp trade (as described in the section on Industry) which improved further in a ten year boom period from 1803, and resulted in a small increase in population. Unfortunately, when the boom ended, people were left destitute and emigration began again.

From 1814 onwards, the estate stepped up its efforts to abolish runrig and the large number of small land-holdings which remained. John Paterson, a new and equally ruthless Factor took over management of the 10th Duke's estate. His plans for the island have been well documented and need not be detailed, except to say that many more large and medium sized farms were to be created and sheep and deer numbers greatly increased. With the exception of a small area around Lochranza, the northern half of the island was to be almost devoid of clachans.

The smaller farms created by Burrel, although they had proved to be viable, were to have their leases refused and combined into larger units. Local farmers could not afford to stock and equip the largest of the farms being created so better-off Ayrshire farmers, versed in the latest methods, were encouraged to settle on Arran. Local men who had had their own land were reduced to labouring for the incomers.

In 1829, Paterson's re-structuring brought the episode which has attracted most attention and is referred to often as if it was the Arran Clearances in their entirety. All of the leases in the north-east corner of the island, roughly from Cock to Corrie, were due for renewal and all were to be refused for the creation of large farms. Around North Sannox, 27 families were evicted to create one farm. The exact number of people evicted at that time is unknown but is likely to have been over 200.

Families were warned in advance that their leases would not be renewed and the Duke made an offer to his tenants - he would pay half of the fare of anyone who emigrated to Canada and would obtain from the Government, a grant of 100 acres of land for each head of a family and for each single man over 21. Many families refused the offer and moved to other parts of Arran or the mainland but some decided on a new way of life in a new country.

On Saturday, 25th April, 1829, twelve families from Sannox area, comprised of 86 adults and children, gathered on the village green at Lamlash. The brig Caledonia was at anchor in the bay, en route from Greenock to Canada. There would be great distress as families and friends took their farewells, knowing they were unlikely to meet again. The Minister of Sannox kirk conducted a brief service, from what tradition says was the hillock still preserved and known as the Preacher's Mound.

The Caledonia arrived at Quebec on 25th June, 1829, but it was the middle of July before the Arran folk arrived at their new lands in Megantic County, about 50 miles south of the St. Lawrence River. Five families who had been unable to get places on the Caledonia, followed in the brig Albion from Greenock on 5th June, 1829 and caught up with the first group at Megantic. The heads of families each received 100 acres, as promised, but the single men got nothing. Clearing and cultivating the virgin land was difficult but for families who had existed by toiling on small strips of land on Arran, the possession of a large acreage must have been a consolation.

The clachan of Auchencar, late in the 19th century.

Between 1830 and 1843, 17 more Arran families emigrated to Megantic, and further emigration over several years brought the ex-Arran population to about 400. Readers who would like to pursue the story of the families in Canada can do so in the book 'Annals of Megantic,' written in 1902 by Dugald MacKillop whose parents were among the emigrants.

In Lamlash, close to the Preacher's Mound, a modern monument commemorates the departure of the Sannox families in 1829. Praiseworthy as the monument is, the most moving memorials are the grass-grown mounds of rubble which mark the sites of the clachans where many generations of people lived out their lives before the Clearances.

Evictions continued for 20 years or more. In the 1840's, for example, 12 cottages, now known as the Twelve Apostles, were built at Catacol for families being removed from Glen Catacol to make way for deer. The landowner had tried to lessen the distress of displacement but the people moved away rather than occupy the houses.

Of the many Arran families displaced by the Clearances one has attracted public attention. Although

The Clearances Monument, Lamlash

many generations of his ancestors had lived in runrig communities at Lochranza, Cock and North Sannox, Daniel MacMillan was born in 1813 on a runrig farm at Achag, above Corrie, where his father shared a lease. The parents and 10 children lived in a small, cottar's cottage. In 1814, the family lost their share of Achag and moved to Irvine where Daniel's father found work as a carter. Daniel served an apprenticeship as a bookseller in Irvine and Glasgow before moving to England where he started in business as a publisher, founding the firm that was to become the world-renowned publishing house, MacMillan London Ltd. Daniel was the Great Grandfather of Lord (Harold) MacMillan, Prime Minister of Britain from 1957 to 1963.

In the days before democracy, it was the duty of landed families to ensure that advances were introduced and progress maintained on their estates. In this respect, the Dukes of Hamilton failed - while the agrarian revolution was moving ahead apace on their other estates, Arran was left in a slough of practices more akin to the Middle Ages. If changes had been introduced earlier there would have been more opportunity to take stock of the needs of displaced people. Nevertheless, change was inevitable and howsoever it was done it was certain to be painful.

CHURCHES

The ruined ST. BRIDE'S CHAPEL is on the hillside north of Brodick Road, Lamlash, alongside the modern Kilbride Cemetery. Built in the 14th century, and badly damaged by fire during an English raid in 1406, the building was probably in use as Kilbride Parish Church until late in the 18th century. The name of the chapel commemorates Bride or Bridget, a 5th century Irish Saint. It is known that on a visit to Arran in 1498, King James IV of Scotland attended mass, which is likely to have been conducted in St. Bride's Chapel.

The graveyard and modern cemetery around the church contain many headstones of special interest, the oldest dating from 1603, and several sculptured stones of curious design. One grave is thought to be that of James Hamilton, 3rd Earl of Arran, who died in 1609. More modern are the graves of Helen Melland, first wife of Prime Minister Henry Asquith, who died while on holiday in Lamlash in 1891; that of Donald McKelvie, breeder of Arran potatoes; and many war graves.

SANNOX CONGREGATIONAL CHURCH was built in 1822 as an independent 'tabernacle', inspired by the evangelical preaching of the brothers Robert and James Haldane who visited Arran in 1800. The congregation was reduced greatly when the north-east corner of the island was almost denuded of people by the 1829 Clearances (see the section on The Clearances). The emigrants who settled in Megantic County, Canada, built their first place of worship as a replica in wood of Sannox Church.

BRODICK'S ORIGINAL CHURCH is seen in the right forefront of this picture of Glen Shurig. Built in 1839, when most of its congregation lived in Cladach, Glen Shurig and the castle grounds, it was demolished shortly after 1931 when the congregation amalgamated with that of the Church of Scotland, Knowe Road, Brodick; by then, most of the people lived around Invercloy and in Douglas Row. All that remains to show that the old kirk existed are the manse, now Arran Estate Office, and the old graveyard at the junction of The String and the road into Glen Shurig.

KILMORY CHURCH is the oldest place of worship still in use on Arran. Built in 1785, possibly on the site of an earlier church, it was refurbished in 1881. The manse adjacent to the church was built about 1690, with a thatched roof; it was burned down in 1710 but as a substantial part of the original fabric was incorporated into the new building, it can claim to be the oldest inhabited manse in Scotland. In 1705, Anne, Duchess of Hamilton, presented two silver communion cups to the church but they were destroyed in the fire in the manse and in 1711 the Duchess provided two beautiful replacement silver cups; they are inscribed "Communion Cups for Aran 1711". Within the church is the figurehead of the schooner Bessie Arnold which was wrecked on Sliddery shore on 28th December, 1908; some of the crew are buried in the kirkyard.

The ruined CLAUCHAN GLEN PREACHING HOUSE was built in 1805 on the site of a similar meeting place which had been built in 1708. The later building continued in use until St. Molios Church, Shiskine, was opened in 1889. The graveyard dates from the early years of the 18th century and the whole site was probably of religious significance from early Christian times.

ST. MOLIOS STONE was removed from Clauchan Glen graveyard and built into the wall of St. Molios Church, Shiskine, in 1889. The effigy of a tonsured cleric represents an ecclesiastic of the Middle Ages, possibly an Abbot of Saddell Abbey across Kilbrannan Sound. The origin of the stone is not known. The effigy is often wrongly claimed to be of the 6th century St. Molios (see Holy Isle).

THE SCULPTURED STONES which stand in front of Lamlash Parish church are a pillared crucifix and a baptismal font. They were unearthed in the graveyard of St. Bride's Chapel, Lamlash in 1892 and almost certainly came originally from a 13th century monastery on Holy Isle. In full, the crucifix is six feet one inch in height, although much of it is below ground level.

INDUSTRY AND COMMERCE

Nature's skill at hiding her scars fosters the misconception that Arran's beautiful landscape has never been blemished by industry and its ensuing dereliction. In fact, over the centuries several industrial enterprises gave much needed employment to people of the island but left a great deal of pollution in their wake.

The best example of such an industry was the production of iron. From far back in prehistory, the people of Arran smelted their own iron in crude furnaces called 'bloomeries', their raw material being ore obtained from bogs, beaches and outcropping seams.

A bloomery was a saucer-shaped depression, between 6 and 10 feet in diameter and lined with clay and stone. It was filled with iron ore, over which charcoal was heaped.

The pile was then clothed in turf and stone, except for air vents, and the charcoal was ignited. When the ore had melted and the iron separated from the slag, the material on top was removed and the still malleable iron hammered into a ball shaped lump called a 'bloom'. The iron was then passed to the blacksmith for further hammering and shaping into tools, implements and domestic items.

Most of the bloomeries were high on hillsides, close to a burn and to woodland. On the hill, they were more likely to get a draught of wind, the burn gave water to cool the slag, and extensive areas of woodland were cut down and converted into charcoal, itself a filthy process. As the bloomeries were in use for hundreds of years, vast quantities of slag, ash and other debris were created, all of

Monamore Meal Mill

which was dumped on the hillside, defiling and disfiguring large areas. Large quantities were removed for road building in the 19th century and Nature has had time to camouflage the remainder.

There were bloomeries at Kilpatrick; Largybeg; Lochranza; Glenkiln; Cnoc Dubh, high above Blairbeg; Auchareoch; and on the ridge between Glen Shurig and Glen Rosa. Production stopped when wood became scarce and mass-produced iron could be obtained easily from the mainland.

Another industry which gave work to many generations of Arran people but made a mess of the immediate environment was the production of kelp.

Kelp is the ash obtained by burning the seaweed of the same name. It contains carbonate of soda which was used in glass- and soap-making. Gathering the seaweed was arduous; apart from the rocky shores at the south-east corner of the island, where most of the kelp was produced, the best places for suitable seaweed were Holy Isle and Pladda, and men went out in smacks to collect it from these islands. Twelve tons of seaweed had to be gathered, laid out to dry, brought together again, and burned to produce one ton of kelp. Permission to gather seaweed had to be obtained from the estate and those who produced kelp had to supply one ton to the Duke annually in part-payment of rent, at a price decided by the Factor. If it was not supplied or was thought to be of inferior quality, twice the current value was added to the producer's rent.

In spite of its drawbacks, kelp production helped to keep many families on the island during the Clearances. A ten year boom in the price of kelp from 1803, slowed emigration and allowed the island's population to rise but when it ended many families were left destitute and emigration started again. From then, kelp production declined steadily and stopped after a few years.

Nature's ability to cover her man-made scars has

enabled Corrie and Sannox to be the picturesque villages we know today, disguising the fact that during the 19th and into the 20th centuries they were industrialised.

In Corrie, the excavation of limestone from the hillside behind the port, together with the quarrying of red sandstone from the south end of the village and white sandstone from the hillside above, must have produced enough noise, debris and dust to pollute the environment. A village thrang with quarrymen, stonemasons and sailors would be obstructed by lines of bogies clattering along on light railways, carrying stone to the harbour and quay.

Intermittently, between 1840 and 1938, barytes was mined in Glen Sannox, and must have produced in Sannox the adverse effects that quarrying had on Corrie, though to a lesser degree. The remains of a concrete hopper at the north end of the village, the quay, and traces of a light railway in the Glen, are reminders of an industrial past.

Other quarrying operations on the island included limestone in Clauchan Glen and red sandstone at Brodick, Cordon and Monamore Glen.

During the 18th and 19th centuries, several other small industries gave employment on the island. In the 1770's, slate was quarried at Glen Farm, Lochranza, several thousand roofing tiles being produced, many of which are likely still to be in use in the district, but the operation lasted for only a few years. About the same time, and equally short lived, was the extraction of coal from shallow or outcropping seams at the Cock. From 1780 to 1840, Pirnmill had a mill for producing wooden pirns (bobbins), hence the name of the village that grew

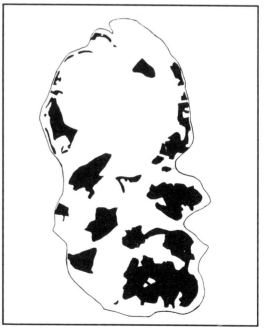

Afforestation of Arran - 1993

around it. There were lime kilns and salt pans at various parts of the island. Lamlash had a mill for wauking and dyeing cloth, Lagg a flax mill, and Brodick and Birican had mills for carding wool. Early in the 19th century there were five meal mills on the island but before the end of the century only those at Shedog and Monamore remained.

In recent years, several good commercial enterprises have been started and, although most of them are not large employer's of labour, between them they make a great contribution to the island's economy.

FORESTRY

Forestry operations have affected the landscape of Arran more than anything has done since the ice age. Vast areas of hillside have been overwhelmed by a blanket of alien pine. Nevertheless, all is not negative; there is a new beauty now in the changing shades and colours of the later, better designed plantations, and the Forestry Commission has provided many facilities for the public.

The Commission began planting in 1952, in Glenrichard, on the south side of the Cloy Burn. As the operation spread throughout the island, the deep-ploughed peaty furrows required for planting young trees were an affront to the island's scenic grandeur, and there was a great deal of public concern. It took several years to hide the scarring and then other problems appeared. Severe geometrical blocks of even-aged trees had turned most of the lower slopes into featureless, monotoned landscapes; well known viewpoints had been obstructed and access was blocked to many popular areas.

To its credit, the Forestry Commission responded to public opinion with improved plantation design which combined trees of mixed species, colour and maturity. Viewpoints were opened up and recreation facilities provided, including the creation of 20 miles of forest roads, 32 miles of walks, 10 miles of cycle routes, 2 picnic sites, and 2 large car parks. A forest walk leaflet was produced and during 1992, Loch Nan Ime on Clauchland Hills was re-created as a wildlife habitat.

Large scale planting stopped in 1989, by which time 16 million trees had been planted on 8,000 hectares of land. Selective harvesting began in 1987. About 3,000 tons of timber are being extracted annually and output is being increased steadily with an anticipated annual production of 100,000 tons by 2007.

The Commission has tried to allay public concern over the effects of extensive harvesting with an assurance that well-planned extraction and immediate re-planting will safeguard Arran's scenic splendour.

During 1992, the Forestry Commission was split into two bodies, the Forestry Authority and Forest Enterprise.

ARRAN PROVISIONS LTD.

Arran Provisions Ltd. is the island's greatest success story of modern times, probably of all time. With production and control confined to the island, the firm has risen from humble beginnings to having a multi-million pound turnover.

Ian and Janet Russell moved to Arran from

Harvesting of the forest - 1992

*Ian Russell and Princess of Wales
at opening of new Monamore factory in 1989*

semi-derelict Home Farm buildings, Brodick. Ian gave up his position with Arran Provisions and in 1990, with a third Director, Janet Murrie, they started a new company called Arran Aromatics to produce a range of toiletries for the gift market. Part of the renovated building houses a small factory and office for the new firm and the remainder has been opened as an attractive visitor centre. Arran Aromatics' products are already carrying the island's name to many countries.

ARRAN CHEESE

The first creamery on Arran was started by the Scottish Milk Marketing Board about 1934 at Bennecarrigan Farm, near the south end of the Ross Road. By buying all of the milk surplus to the island's liquid milk consumption, the Board brought stability to Arran farmers' incomes.

Until the creamery was opened, cheese was made on almost every dairy farm on the island but after the creamery started the production of farmhouse cheese declined and now all Arran cheese is produced commercially.

In 1944, the S.M.M.B. moved their operation to a new creamery at Torrylin, Kilmory, from which it operates still.

Torrylin creamery receives about 2.8 million litres of milk from Arran's farms annually, from which it produces about 270 tons of Dunlop type cheese. About 70 tons of the output is used to make the individually packed 1 lb and 2 lb cheeses which have proved to be very popular in the island's gift trade as well as in the normal retail market. In addition to the U.K., orders are exported regularly to

Birmingham in 1973 and took over the Old Pier Shop, Whiting Bay. They had no business experience, Ian having been a policeman and Janet a nurse. Both had been born in England but Ian's forebears were from Corrie and Arran had always been part of his life.

The Pier Shop business included petrol pumps and soon Ian started hiring bicycles, as his grandfather had done in Corrie about 70 years earlier. Business was too seasonal but Ian had an idea for a sideline, an idea which most people would have laughed at - they would make and market mustard. In 1979, in the kitchen of their home, they began producing an unusual seedy mustard which they called The Original Arran Mustard. The product was sold in attractive ceramic jars with the name Arran prominently displayed and it was an immediate success in the island's gift trade. The Arran Mustard company was formed and a small factory built at Monamore, Lamlash. Soon, several unusual varieties of mustard were being produced and the range expanded to include jams, jellies and preserves, all with the Arran prefix in the names. The company name was changed to Arran Provision Ltd. and soon Arran goods were on sale throughout the U.K., Europe, North America and Japan. Several million jars of the products were being produced annually and the firm had an annual turnover of around £4 million.

In 1985, the Russells sold out their company but production remained on the island and Ian stayed on as Managing Director. In 1989, the Princess of Wales opened new factory premises at Monamore. Staff numbers vary seasonably between 50 and 110.

Meantime, the Russells had bought and renovated the

Neil McLean, Manager in Torrylin Creamery

The staff of the Arran Banner, 1993

The Banner is now an integral part of life on Arran and copies are posted each week to subscribers throughout the U.K. and in New Zealand, Australia, Canada, the U.S.A., France, Germany, Belgium, Norway, Sweden, and to the Royal Palace at Monaco. The paper is in the Guinness Book of Records as the British weekly newspaper read by the highest percentage of people in its area, reckoned to be about 97+% of the people of Arran.

The Arran Banner's archives are already a treasure store of information on matters which have affected the lives of ordinary people on the island and no social history of Arran during the past twenty years could be compiled without reference to them.

FISH FARMING

Fish farming off Arran was started in 1983 by Howard and Rosemary Walker of Lamlash who reared salmon and trout in two pens in Lamlash Bay. In 1987, they sold out to Marine Harvest Ltd., an international company who own most of Scotland's fish farms. The company started their Arran operation with a group of ten fish pens and expanded in 1989 with two more groups of ten pens. In 1990, the shore base was moved from Lamlash to Kingscross. Originally, the Marine Harvest farm was a production site, harvesting 500 tons of fish annually but now it is the company's main 'bloodstock' site, producing eggs from pedigree salmon for the company's world-wide operations.

ARRAN TRANSPORT AND TRADING COMPANY carries the island's name throughout the U.K. and to continental Europe. The company has grown steadily since Robert and Margaret Haddow came to Arran in 1963 and

the U.S.A., Germany, France, Belgium, occasionally to Turkey, and recently to Hong Kong.

Torrylin creamery which employs six people has won many important awards, including first prizes at the London Dairy Show. In the last three years, it has won Scotland's top award in its class twice and was placed second in the third year.

THE ARRAN BANNER

The first Arran Banner came out in March, 1974. It was produced in Whiting Bay by a group of enthusiastic amateurs and printed by one of their number called Paul Monty. If there was insufficient material, friends were asked to submit letters and when the printed pages had to be folded and brought together, the group and friends held all-night 'collating parties'.

The paper was produced only monthly but by the end of 1976 initial enthusiasm had faded and production was about to end when Ronnie Mann, a local businessman took it over. He moved production to Brodick and, assisted by a friend, Marc Head, operated the business on a proper financial basis. The paper was produced weekly and after a year circulation had increased to about 1,000 copies in winter and between 1,600 and 1,800 in summer.

In December, 1980, the Banner was sold to its present proprietors, John and Deanna Miller. They had had no previous experience of working on or producing a newspaper but by applying themselves to the many and varied tasks involved, they steadily increased circulation to the present figures of 2,400 in winter and 3,500 in summer.

Fish Farm staff, 1993

bought over part of Lennox Motor Services. Mr. Haddow had been born on Arran but brought up in Glasgow. Soon, they acquired more of Arran's 'bus and transport firms and within a few years Arran Transport and Trading Company was providing all of the island's buses and most of its haulage services. Now, the firm's vehicles are well known all over Britain. About 1970, to employ drivers during slack periods, the company started digging and selling local sand to the island's builders and now this part of the business has expanded greatly and, as the Filtration Supplies and Services Company, sells and transports Arran sand to many parts of Britain, Europe, Africa and the Middle East. The sand is of a grade suitable for water filtration, but in the public perception it takes acumen to sell sand to the Arabs. Based at Brodick Pier, the Haddows employ up to 50 people and make a great contribution to the island's economy.

AN ARRAN MISCELLANY

THE TRAVELLING PEOPLE. No history of Arran would be complete without reference to the travelling people who came from Kintyre and spent the summer months on the island. Commonly, and not unkindly, called the tinkers, many generations of McPhees, Townsleys, MacAlisters and other families were well known to all locals. Travelling with their horse-drawn or hand carts, they set up camp with their familiar 'humpy' tents on the same sites year after year, as they sought casual work on farms or sold their wares from door to door. In the 1970's a permanent site with good facilities was established at Merkland Wood, north of Brodick, and since then casual camping has been prohibited.

TELEGRAPH AND TELEPHONE SERVICES. The telegraph poles in the 1904 view from Whiting Bay pierhead, looking north to Arnhall, is a reminder that telegraph and telephone services came reasonably early to Arran. The first telegraph was installed in Brodick post office in 1872 and operated by Miss Ribbeck, Postmistress. Soon, it was extended all over the island and a full-time linesman was appointed in 1886. The first telephone was installed in 1891 as a private line between Brodick Castle and Dougarie Lodge, and the first link with the mainland was made in 1913. The building which is now Brodick Chemist's shop was the village post office from 1886 to 1913 and housed the island's first telephone exchange. The photograph below shows the Corrie mail brake, driven by Kaspar Ribbeck, about to leave the post office in 1902.

A horse sale at Brodick Fair in 1905

ARRAN FAIRS. Throughout the 19th century and the first half of the 20th century, Fair Days were holidays for most people. Principally, the fairs were markets for the sale of animals and produce but they were also occasions for socializing, accompanied by simple entertainments. By the middle of the 19th century, Arran had fairs at Lamlash, Brodick, Lagg and Shedog (2). The 'Kirktoun o' Kilbride' Fair on Lamlash green was the most ancient but was in decline and stopped before the end of the century. Those at Lagg and Shedog were small events, mainly for the sale of horses, but were important socially. Brodick Fair had been going for only a few years but was already the most popular. The fair of 1847 was described as occupying a quarter of a mile of the public road and two fields close to the shore, although the exact location was not given. There were numerous refreshment tents, an abundance of stalls, gambling games and penny dances. In the evening, the locals held 'athletic games'. Four fully laden steamers brought visitors from the mainland, even although it was 25 years before the pier was built. In later years, merry-go-rounds, shooting galleries, fortune tellers and more side-shows were introduced and gradually the original concept of a market was abandoned, but still it attracted visitors from the mainland.

Brodick Fair in the 1920's

A ROYAL VISIT. The 6th Duke of Montrose is pictured welcoming King George VI and Queen Elizabeth, Princesses Elizabeth and Margaret, and Lieutenant Philip Mountbatten as they came ashore on Brodick pier for a royal visit to Arran on 24th July, 1947.

THE WHITEHOUSE stood secluded by its woods, lawns and attractive gardens in the middle of Lamlash, on the site now derelict between the church and Arran High School. Built in the first quarter of the 19th century it was the home of the Estate Factor, John Paterson, known as 'the terror of The Whitehouse'. He was succeeded in the post by his son of the same name who lived in the house until 1881. In later years, it was a dower house for the Dowager Duchess of Hamilton, and finally, for its last forty years was a hotel with public bars. It was demolished in 1982 to make way for development that has not yet taken place.

THE ISLE OF ARRAN HERITAGE MUSEUM, Rosaburn, Brodick, is set in a group of 18th century croft buildings which include a semi-detached cottage, a bothy, a smiddy and a composite coach-house, stable and harness room. The idea for an island museum was conceived by the late Miss Bess MacMillan M.B.E. of Brodick. In 1976, the Isle of Arran Museum Association and the Isle of Arran Museum Trust were formed and in the same year the first group of buildings at Rosaburn were acquired. The museum was opened to the public in 1979 and extended in 1981 by the acquisition of more buildings on the site. The Museum Association and Museum Trust are non-profitmaking bodies, run by Arran people on a voluntary basis. The Trust has charitable status and is funded by entrance fees, membership subscriptions from the Association, and grants from various organisations.

THE ARRAN SUFFRAGETTE

Flora Drummond, nee Gibson (1879-1949) was born at Pirnmill. On one side of her family she was related to Charles Robertson and his daughter, Mrs. Kathy Rankin, who between them ran Pirnmill Post Office from 1891 to 1958; on the other side, she was related to the Cook family who originally operated the Pirnmill ferry. Flora trained as a telegraphist and, hoping to be a post mistress, sat and passed the Civil Service examinations, but failed to obtain an appointment because she was under the regulation height of 5'2". She moved to Manchester to work as a typist and joined the Women's Social and Political Union, which was leading the national campaign for women's suffrage. Flora followed Mrs. Emmeline Pankhurst, the suffragette leader, to London and became the organiser of the movement's demonstrations. Dressed in uniform and on horseback, she led most of the vast marches in the capital and became known as 'The General'. With her knowledge of telegraphy, she organized suffragette intelligence in Holloway prison by having messages tapped in code on the pipes between the cells.

JEANIE HERING (1851-1928) and her husband, John Adams-Acton, a sculptor, are commemorated on a sculptured column in Brodick's old graveyard. Baptised Marion Hamilton, Jeanie was the daughter of a Brodick girl and, according to rumour, one of the local Ducal family. As a child she was adopted by an English artist called Hering who changed her name. It was for Hering that the 11th Duke had the house 'Ormidale' built in Brodick. In 1886, Jeanie created an Arran legend when, with her six children - one a year old infant in a perambulator - and two maids, she walked from London to Glasgow, en route to a family holiday on Arran. The walk took about five weeks of a wet summer. One of the maids, Ellen, married John Sillars, later of West Mayish Farm, and died in 1958, aged 95.

The remains of DUCHESS ANNE'S HARBOUR, Lamlash, can be seen south of the old pier at low tide. The Duchess of Hamilton, known on the island as Good Duchess Anne, had the harbour built late in the 17th century at a cost of £2913. Tradition maintains she intended the construction of the harbour to give much needed employment to the men of the area. By 1772, the harbour was a ruin and its stones were being used for house-building in the village. The red sandstone blocks can be seen in the walls of houses nearby.

BRODICK PIER OFFICE and waiting room shown was a familiar landmark for several generations. Designed by J.J. Burnett, it was built as a single-storey building in 1899, with an upper storey being added to the landward end later. The building was demolished in November, 1993, on completion of the new offices and waiting area.

ARRAN'S POP CONCERT. On 13th July 1991, Arran was the focus of nationwide media attention when, due to the influence of local girl, Jackie Brambles, and the generosity of the Scottish pop group, Wet Wet Wet, a full broadcasting roadshow, complete with a huge canopied stage, gave a free concert in Lamlash. Enthusiasts converged on the island from many parts of Britain and Ireland and formed a well-behaved audience, variously estimated at between 5,000 and 10,000, and was, certainly, the largest attendance, by far, at any event ever held on Arran.

A TRAVELLING LADY on the Machrie road with her worldly possessions in and old pram. Although the undated photograph is fairly modern, such women were a familiar sight as they tramped the island roads, especially during the depression years between the wars. They lived rough, sleeping wherever they could find shelter, but many kept themselves clean and tidy. By selling threads, pins and needles, and other small items around the farms and villages, they earned a meagre income but depended upon people's kindness for most of their needs.

THE ROADMEN'S TAR BOILERS were a familiar sight and smell between the 1920's and 80's as they were towed around the island, boiling tar for surfacing the roads. Barrels of tar were brought to the island by 'Puffer' and, when required were stacked against the hot boiler to make their contents easier to pour. Some mothers of 'chesty' children took them to a tar boiler, in the belief that the pungent fumes were good for 'clearing the tubes'. Boys moulded warm tar into a ball at the end of a piece of string, hardened it in cold water, and used the 'taury ba·' as a conker. The men in the 1971 photograph are Donald Stewart, Corriecravie; Donald Sim, Shannochie; and the late Donald MacKenzie, Kilmory.

THE RESCUE SERVICES

ARRAN MOUNTAIN RESCUE TEAM was formed in 1964. At present it has 28 members and two search and rescue dogs. All of the members are volunteers, drawn from around the island and from a wide variety of occupations. Strathclyde Police provide communication equipment and transport, otherwise, except for occasional small grants, the team is supported by local fund raising projects. The team has rescued in excess of 150 people from accidents in the hills, assisted in numerous searches for missing persons, and recovered many trapped animals.

AN R.N.L.I. INSHORE RESCUE BOAT has been stationed on Arran since 1970. An inflatable craft and rescue equipment are held at the Old Pier, Lamlash, but the crew of 15 are divided between Lamlash and Shiskine. The volunteer crews have attended numerous emergencies at sea over the years and have saved several lives.

AUXILIARY COASTGUARDS trained for sea and cliff rescues, have operated on Arran since the start of this century, and possibly earlier. A vehicle and rescue equipment are held at their base in Lamlash but the 16 volunteer members are spread between Lamlash, Kildonan and Lochranza. The unit is responsible for co-ordinating all helicopter mercy missions to the island, other than mountain rescue flights.

FIRE BRIGADE units have operated on the island since 1939. There are units at Lamlash, Brodick, Lochranza, Blackwaterfoot and Corriecravie, the first two being retained units and the others volunteer units. The photograph is of Brodick Brigade in the 1940's with their senior officer, Jimmy Gordon of Lamlash (back right).

PLADDA LIGHTHOUSE is the second oldest in the firth of Clyde. Built first in 1790, it was re-built in 1825. The smaller tower shown in the photograph was added c. 1800 to create a double light and distinguish it from the Little Cumbrae and Mull of Kintyre lights; it was discontinued in 1901.

PILLAR ROCK LIGHTHOUSE (Holy Isle), built in 1905, was the first square-towered lighthouse, designed to eliminate the need for interior fittings to follow the contours of round towers. It was erected to supplement the other Holy Isle light which was not visible from the north.

HOLY ISLE LIGHTHOUSE (opposite Kingscross Point) was built in 1877. In 1894, the lightkeepers received nationwide publicity for rescuing the Captain and crew of the vessel 'Ossian' which was wrecked nearby. When the Samye Ling Buddhists bought the island in 1992, they took over the lightkeeper's houses.

THE AIR SEA RESCUE HELICOPTERS AND CREWS of H.M.S. Gannet, Monkton, have been part of life on Arran for over a quarter of a century. They have co-operated with the island's civilian rescue services in real and simulated rescues on mountain, sea and shore; emergency medical cases have been transported to mainland hospitals; and displays have been given during village gala weeks.

AGRICULTURE

The history of agriculture in Arran could not be summarised in a section of this book in any way appropriate to the industry's importance to the island. Since Neolithic man first settled to the tasks of clearing land, growing crops and domesticating animals, farming has been the most important of all industries for mankind. By providing food, it has fuelled all of man's progress and, as improved methods of agriculture have increased the quantity and variety of food, the quality and expectancy of life has been enhanced for the mass of the people. Unfortunately, for the people of Arran, these advances were much later in being attained than they were in most of the kingdom.

Land-management and basic farming methods were allowed to stagnate on Arran from the Middle Ages to the last quarter of the 18th century. All but a few of the people lived in groups of dwellings called clachans. Each clachan had a Tacksman who held the lease of the clachan land, collected rents from his neighbours, and paid the full rent to the landowner. Other than Cottars, who laboured to those with land, each family had a share of the clachan land. No land was enclosed by dykes or hedges.

Agriculture was based on the ancient celtic runrig system. The complexities of runrig need to be understood by only the historian or the student of agronomy. Basically,

the land around a clachan was divided into two parts, the infield, close at hand and generally in a valley floor or on the lower slopes of hills, and the outfield on the higher, rougher land. The infield was divided into hump-backed strips, called rigs, which were allocated by drawing lots annually or biennially. Normally, a family's rigs were not adjacent to each other and had to be accessed by trudging round neighbours' holdings. Cattle had to be herded to the more distant outfield, where land was held communally and individual rights related to the number of animals allowed to be grazed. The limited extent of each family's holding and the frequent re-allocation of rigs, discouraged long-term measures to improve the soil and regulate crop rotation. All-in-all, farming was not a business, as we know it; each family produced enough to enable it to subsist, hopefully with a little extra to sell to let them pay their rent and replace their animals. Nevertheless, their limited right to a small land-holding within the runrig system was all of consequence that most families possessed and they were unlikely to forego their place in the system voluntarily. Without an end to runrig, allowing larger parcels of land and longer tenure, agriculture on Arran could not be improved.

The introduction of new land-management systems by the Duke of Hamilton's Factors, which started in 1772

Simmental cow 'Arran Clova' and calf, winners of the overhead championship at Arran Farmers' Society show in 1990 for D. & M. Currie, Birchburn, Shiskine.

and continued intermittently until the middle of the 19th century (see the Section on The Clearances), brought an end to runrig and the communal holding of land, and allowed the introduction of modern methods of agriculture, which included the approach to farming as a business. Arran Farmers' Society was founded in 1830 and it did a great deal to enlighten and encourage the island's farmers in the use of new methods, new crops and the better breeding of livestock. Before the end of the 19th century, Arran's farms were efficient and their produce renowned.

The setting up in 1933 of the Scottish Milk Marketing Board gave dairy farmers a guaranteed outlet for their milk and introduced a substantial measure of stability and security at a time when the industry was in the doldrums. In the second half of this century, farming has been characterised by state intervention, intensive cultivation, maximized productivity and mechanisation, the last-mentioned resulting in a dramatic reduction in manpower. In recent years, farms have been combined into larger holdings, small farms are barely viable, and crofting has been reduced to hobby status.

To the layman, one of the saddest results of modern farming conditions is the reversion to a state much wilder than Nature would have managed on her own, of so many fields which generations of men with only rude implements slaved to make arable.

One consequence of modern technology which some of Arran's farmers could well have done without was the insidious radioactive contamination of their land in 1986, caused by the nuclear explosion at Chernoby 11500 miles away as the crow flies. On two farms, restrictions on the movement of sheep were not lifted until January 1994.

Incongruously, Arran's most famous contribution to agriculture was not due to the work of a farmer but of a shopkeeper. As the name Clydesdale is to horses and Ayrshire is to dairy cattle, so Arran has been to potatoes, due to the efforts of Donald McKelvie, O.B.E.

Mr. McKelvie was descended from one of the island's oldest families. His roots were in Kildonan but he spent most of his young life in Glasgow. He qualified as a Chartered Accountant but in 1894, aged 28, succeeded to a grocery business in Lamlash and returned to live in the village. The business, D. McNeish & Son, occupied the premises now owned by the S.C.W.S.

About 1901, a friend gave Donald McKelvie some seed potatoes but he did not know how to grow them. With advice, he grew his potatoes and soon 'drifted into' dealing in fairly large quantities as a side-line to his business. In 1906, an English potato merchant sent him six packets of potato seed and from then until the end of his life he bred potatoes, becoming the best-known breeder of his day and far beyond.

The name 'Arran' was seen first on a potato in 1911 when McKelvie marketed a main crop variety called Arran Chief. It was a major success, proving to be very popular, especially in Ireland where it was grown widely

Donald McKelvie with samples of Arran potatoes

61

for the next thirty years or more. In 1917, he marketed a new variety called Arran Treasure which became popular quickly in England but he considered it unworthy of the 'Arran' prefix and withdrew it from sale. In 1919, he put it back on the market called Ally and it won him his first Gold Medal in trials in England.

Success continued regularly with other 'Arran' varieties:- Comrade (1918); Rose (1918); Victory (1918); Consul (1924); Banner (1926); Crest (1928); Pilot (1930); Scout (1930); Cairn (1932); Signet (1936); Peak (1936); and Viking (1945); eight of them winning Gold Medals. Other varieties, in unknown years, were Arran Bard, Arran Comet, Arran Luxury and Arran Scot.

Donald McKelvie was never a farmer, he was a shopkeeper with an absorbing hobby, He cultivated only 25 acres of land, most of it on the south and east side of Lamlash public park . In sheds behind his shop and in a large greenhouse at Claveron, Lamlash, he grew as many as 3,000 first year plants which had been produced by cross-pollination or grafting. By strict testing, he reduced the numbers annually until, after six or seven years, he was left with less than ten. Plants which reached the third year were planted out in trial plots to test their yield and resistance to disease. Varieties which survived and which he judged to have commercial possibilities were distributed among colleagues in various parts of Britain and Ireland to have them tried in other soil and climatic conditions. After all the painstaking work, in many years there was no new variety worth marketing.

At a dinner in his honour in Douglas Hotel, Brodick in 1925, attended by farmers and business men from all from all over the U.K., Donald McKelvie was presented

Donald McKelvie with some of his ponies
on the site now occupied by Arran High School

with his portrait in oils. As he was unmarried (and remained so), there was an understanding that on his death the portrait would pass to the West of Scotland Agricultural College, Auchencruive, where it is kept together with his Gold Medals.

As hundreds of breeders and several research

establishment are continually producing new varieties of potato, it is not surprising that most of McKelvies 'Arran' varieties have been superseded. It is a tribute to its quality that 63 years after it was introduced, Arran Pilot is still popular with gardeners. Arran Banner, bred 67 years ago and possibly the heaviest cropping main crop potato of all time, was the most popular variety with Cypriot growers until 1989, and there is renewed interest in the purple skinned Arran Victory of 1918. Maris Piper, the most popular British potato of the last thirty years, was bred from Arran Cairn.

Donald McKelvie was also an internationally known breeder of Highland ponies, won all of the breed's major awards, and exported ponies from his Lamlash stud to several foreign countries including Palestine and Argentina.

The Lady Jean Fforde welcomes the Princess Royal
to the 150th Agricultural Show on 28th July, 1986

'Boss' McKelvie, as he was known locally, died at this home , 'New Lanark', Lamlash on 30th March 1947 aged 81, and was buried in Kilbride cemetery on the edge of the village. For his contribution to food production, he had been awarded the O.B.E. in 1945. No man has ever spread the name of Arran wider.

COUNTRY LIFE

THE MILKMAID is wearing a coarse apron, which at the time would be called a brat, and carrying a luggie, a wooden pail with extended staves, used for hand-milking. When a cow had calved, the second and third batches of milk, called beesty or beestings, were thick and strong tasting. It was heated until it became granular curds in whey which was eaten as a highly flavoured meal.

HAYMAKING AT LARGYBEG late in the 1800's, with the bearded farmer, Sandy Thomson, in the centre of the picture. The girls were sisters, boarded out by the local authority. For about a hundred years until the Second World War, young people of both sexes in local authority care were boarded out with farming families who were paid for their accommodation and food while the authority supplied their clothing and other basic necessities. These boarders had to work for scant reward. On most farms, they were well treated and many stayed on long after they were eligible to leave but some were harshly treated and over-worked as no more than cheap labour.

THE TRADESMAN'S VAN was an essential part of country life during the long period between the end of almost total self-sufficiency, when people had to subsist mainly on what they could produce themselves, and the 20th century's ease of access to a wide range of shops and food. Vanmen travelled long distances in all weathers.

SPINNING AND CARDING WOOL was done by the womenfolk, while operating the heavy weaving looms was men's work. In many families, hand-knitting was shared by both sexes. Groups of women often came together to card and spin, probably the forerunner of ladies' sewing-bees. The picture was taken at Knockenkelly, late in the 19th century.

TRAMPING THE WASHING in a wooden tub, sometimes called a bine, was a regular part of domestic life and a task enjoyed by the children. The photograph was taken at the south end of Arran in the 1890's.

Robert Currie, THE LAST BLACKSMITH AT ROSABURN, at the door of his workshop which is now part of the Isle of Arran Heritage Museum. In every village and scattered community, the smiddy was a meeting-place in which men gathered to exchange news and views. The blacksmith was depended upon for many tasks, ranging from shoeing horses to ringing wooden cart wheels, repairing machinery and tools, making girdles for baking and 'girds and cleeks' as toys for children. The smiddy operated until the 1960's.

WASHING DAY AT KNOCKENKELLY, complete with 'running water' and the latest in 'washing machines'. Clothes and napery were boiled in the coal or peat fired copper boiler and steeped in the large wooden tubs.

If the boiler could be located near water, as in the photograph, it saved a great deal of carrying. Although the photograph was taken late in the 19th century, such domestic circumstances were commonplace until well into the 20th century.

ARRAN'S LAST BLANKET WEAVERS were the Campbells of The Slochd. The family are pictured in front of their home which is now a ruin alongside Bridge Farm, Ballymichael. The weaving of blankets was a common cottage industry until the middle of the 19th century when mass production in factories gave a wider range of products at cheaper prices. Locally woven blankets were notable for their durability but not for their attractiveness.

AN ARRAN CROFTER late in the 19th century. Although mechanical reaping had become steadily more common in Scotland from the 1850's and the string-tying sheaf binder from the 1890's, such innovations were far beyond the means of Arran's crofters and small farmers, for most of whom the scythe was the means of cutting hay and cereal crops well into the 20th century. A man with a scythe could cut about two acres in a ten hour day, followed by his women folk who gathered, tied and stooked the sheaves. It was all back-breaking labour and one must wonder how the womenfolk coped in their thick, cumbersome clothing.

ROADS AND TRANSPORT

Too often in the study of local history, insufficient attention is paid to the vital subjects of roads and transport. Without a tolerable road system and an efficient means of transport, no part of any land can be developed properly - industrially, commercially or sociologically.

In reviewing how Arran's road system evolved, it is not necessary to delve into the long history of road making as significant improvement did not take place on the island until less than 200 years ago.

Until late in the 17th century, there were no man-made roads on Arran. People travelled on foot or on horseback on a network of well-trodden tracks. In addition to the obvious routes on or near beaches, the island had many tracks across the high muirs, the longest of which included those from Lamlash by Benlister Glen and Clauchan Glen to Shiskine; Lochranza by the Boguille to Sannox; Lochranza by Cock and Laggan to Sannox; Glenree to Feorline and Shiskine; Brodick by Glen Shurig and Gleann ant-Suidhe to Shiskine and Machrie; and Monamore by Auchareoch to Kilmory. Many of the beach tracks were not passable at high tide and the many

burns which had to be waded or crossed by stepping stones hampered travel when in spate. Loads had to be carried or transported in panniers on pack-horses. All in all, travel was generally travail.

During the last few years of the 1600's, the island's first three man-made roads were constructed. One ran up Clauchan Glen to the limestone quarries at its head. The second went up Glen Shurig and down Gleann An T-Suidhe to Shiskine, on the hillsides opposite those on which The String was constructed a century later. The third was between Lamlash Bay and Brodick Bay; its route has not been recorded but it is likely to have left Lamlash by Blairbeg or Blairmore and to have approached Brodick by Mayish. The roads would be narrow, without foundations, and liable to be washed away by heavy rain; by present standards they would be very primitive.

In 1810, Arran's first road suitable for a wheeled vehicle was built, although there were still very few vehicles of that type on the island. The road ran for five miles from Gortonallister, south of Lamlash, to Brodick, and whilst it was much better than the old road, it was still

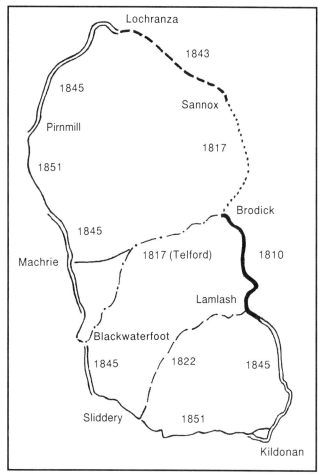

The development of Arran's road system.
Reproduced from Mitchell-Luker's Arran Bus Book.

Dougarie Ford about 1920

rough, narrow and without foundations. There were no stone bridges, only wooden footbridges across a few of the burns. Seven years later, the road was extended across the island to the shore at Blackwaterfoot, by The String, planned by the famous engineer, Thomas Telford. About the same time, the Duke of Hamilton had a road constructed from the Brodick end of The String to Sannox, and in 1822 the Ross Road was built from Lamlash to Sliddery.

This ended the first phase of modern road building on Arran. The central parts of the island, east and west, had taken a great step forward in their development, into an era of improved trade, communications, transport and accessibility. Unfortunately, only about six villages benefited fully. During the following few years, short stretches of new road were constructed at Kilpatrick, Largybeg and Auchencairn but another thirty-odd years were to pass before all of the island's road system was completed.

Even when new roads were available, people did not abandon quickly the tracks they had used for so long, as is shown in an account of a visit to the island in the 1830's. The Rev. Dr. David Landsborough, Minister of Stevenston, disembarked at Lamlash on a June evening, accompanied by a young man he had met on the boat and who was making his way home to Shiskine. Together, in the gloaming, they walked up Benlister Glen, across the high muirland, and down Clauchan Glen, the Minister stumbling along in the wake of his companion. It was midnight before the Minister reached his lodging at Shiskine.

A few years later, Rev. Landsborough escorted a young lady on a daytime excursion from Corrie over the Boguille to Lochranza, he walking and she on a pony. Although it was a fine day, the track was so rugged and the descent into Glen Chalmadale so perilous that they chose to return by the much longer and still rugged route across the hill from Lochranza to Laggan and on by the Fallen Rocks to Sannox.

In the summer of 1840, the Minister arranged to holiday with his wife and family in Lochranza and having sailed into Brodick, took a carriage to Corrie. He had been told that a road had been built to Lochranza since his previous visit and found this to be wrong only on his arrival on Arran. At Corrie, he hired a small sailing boat and boatmen to take his wife, two of his children and a servant girl to Lochranza while he and two sons set out to walk. The party met up again at Sannox where the boat could go no further because of a strong headwind.

Leaving their luggage with the boatmen for delivery later, the family set out to walk over the Boguille to Lochranza. The Minister had thought it best to walk round the coast but was persuaded by the boatmen to take the inland route. After walking for two hours, by which time they had lost the track, the weather deteriorated and on the high muirs they faced a strong wind, heavy rain and thick mist. They stumbled on through the heather for two more hours before the mist cleared and the Minister recognised Gleann Easan Biorach, down which they made their way into Lochranza. By the time they reached their lodgings, they had been walking for five hours and were thoroughly soaked, their discomfort compounded by their changes of clothing having been left with the boatmen.

The coast road at Machrie about 1920

The road from Sannox to Lochranza was not built until 1843 and it was 1851 before the last link in the road system was completed, that being from Catacol to Pirnmill over the still hazardous section at Craw. Arran had, by then, almost 90 miles of roads, the same length and mostly on the same alignments as we know at present, but they should not be envisaged as bearing comparison with modern roads. As late as the 1870's, a widely travelled visitor, having walked round the shore from Brodick to Lamlash, was pleased to return by 'the inland road to Brodick, although it proved to be a very rural path among silver birches, and the walking was literally in a watercourse the whole way'.

When heavy horse-drawn vehicles were introduced, most of the roads had to be strengthened and widened, as had to be done again when motor omnibuses came to the island. Most of the stone bridges were not built until between 1890 and 1920, and none of the roads were surfaced with tar until the 1920's.

As with other aspects of its development, road-making on Arran was neglected for too long. As early as 1750, seventy years before Arran had a mere thirty miles of roads, and a century before the island's road system was completed, extensive road and bridge building schemes were underway throughout Lowland Scotland and in the Highlands there were over 1500 miles of roads and more than 1000 stone bridges. Such late provision of roads delayed many forms of development on Arran, not least being the provision of better facilities for its people.

From the last few years of the 18th century there were some light carts on Arran, mainly at the south end, but as the lack of drainage kept the ground soft for most of the year, they were of limited use, even within the confines of a farm. As more roads were constructed, the number of carts would increase, although their size and weight would be curtailed by the poor standard of the roads. These carts were the first form of wheeled vehicle used for carrying people.

The earliest known reference to a 'carriage' being for hire on the

Horse-drawn brake at Kildonan Hotel in 1906.

The first motor car on Arran - 1897

By the 1870's, several horse-drawn coaches were being operated on passenger services, linking various villages and connecting with the steamers. Two family names of operators of the period are still involved in the island's vehicle trade, these being Ribbeck of Brodick and Weir of Machrie. During the 1890's the island became fully covered by a network of passenger transport services and, in addition, many farmers hired out one and two-horse carriages to visitors, as a sideline.

The first motor car to be seen on Arran was brought by a visitor in 1897 and it astonished the locals by travelling the seven miles from Brodick to Sannox in thirty-five minutes. There is doubt about which local was first to own a motor car but it was probably brought to the island shortly before the First World War.

In 1913, Colin Currie of Ballymichael operated the first motor omnibus on Arran. It was a solid tyred, chain driven, open-sided Albion charabanc, able to carry fifteen passengers. Unfortunately, the roads had not been built to carry such a great weight and were badly damaged by the vehicle.

island was in 1840 when, as noted earlier, Rev. Landsborough hired one from Brodick to take his family to Corrie. By then there were over thirty miles of roads on the island and regular steamer services from the mainland, and it would be surprising if some enterprising locals were not plying for hire at Brodick and Lamlash, offering transport to locals and visitors.

The island had a fairly comprehensive coverage of 'bus services by the 1920's, although, even then, horse-drawn carriages assembled at each pierhead for the arrival of a steamer, many of the carriages being owned by the larger hotels.

The 1930's saw the start of a heyday for 'bus operators.

The first omnibus on Arran - 1913

Until the car ferry Glen Sannox was introduced in 1957, vehicles being transported
had to be driven on board across two planks of wood and secured on the open deck.

As few people on Arran owned a car and scarcely any were brought by visitors, almost everyone travelled by 'bus. The Second World War years were a boom period, due to large numbers of service personnel and their families being on the island, an increase in the number of holidaymakers, and the restrictions on petrol for private use. An excellent passenger service was provided all year round.

The beginning of the end of the 'bus heyday was heralded in 1957 when the car ferry Glen Sannox took over the Ardrossan/Brodick run. Car ownership was spreading rapidly, on and off the island, and the number of cars on Arran's roads increased dramatically within a few years. Since then, succeeding ferries have been required to have ever increasing vehicle capacities, indeed, perfectly good vessels have had to be replaced because they could not cope with the vehicle traffic during the summer months.

Larger car decks allowed heavy vehicles to be carried on the ferries and, progressively, road transport took over the carriage of freight to and from the island. As a result, Arran Transport & Trading Company's large commercial vehicles have carried the island's name widely throughout the U.K.

The age of the motor car and large commercial vehicle is with us and can not be ignored. Roads and car parks must be able to cope, nevertheless, such things as dual carriageways, traffic lights and a proliferation of yellow lines would be incongruous on Arran and must be avoided. They would destroy the well-loved character of the island.

Fording the burn at Catacol in the 1920's

LENNOX MOTOR SERVICES was the largest 'bus and car-hire company on the island until taken over by Arran Transport in 1963. The picture, taken outside the firm's Whiting Bay garage in 1924, shows that even then foreign vehicles were popular in Britain. The vehicles are three Buicks, a Minerva and a Fiat 14-seater charbanc. Drivers dressed in jodphurs and knee-length leather boots, like the man on the right in the photography, were a common sight in the transitional period between horse-drawn and motorised vehicles.

Caledonian MacBrayne's M.V. CALEDONIAN ISLES took over the Ardrossan/Arran service during August, 1993. The largest ferry to have been on service on the firth of Clyde, she can transport 1000 passengers and 120 motor cars, and can accommodate the biggest commercial vehicles, a vast increase in both capacity and need since pre-1957.

SPORTS & PASTIMES

THE ARRAN FOOTBALL ASSOCIATION CHALLENGE CUP was presented by the local M.P., The Right Hon. A. Graham Murray (later Lord Dunedin) in 1903. It is a replica of the Scottish Football Association Cup, except that it has lost the small figure of a footballer from the top of its lid. Since it was presented, the cup has been competed for annually by village and district teams from all over the island. The first winners were Corrie, with a team composed largely of Miners from the barytes mines in Glen Sannox. The island teams also participate annually in an Arran football league.

AN ARRAN SELECT FOOTBALL TEAM including players from various teams on the island, chosen to play a charity match against an Ayrshire Old Crocks XI in 1988.

ARRAN RUGBY FOOTBALL CLUB was formed early in the 1970's after challenge matches had been played between teams from various parts of the island. An island team was selected and matches played against mainland clubs, visiting naval crews, and touring teams from England. After a few years, the club joined Division II of the Glasgow and District Rugby Leagues and soon gained promotion to Division I. During the 1980's, the team was fortunate to be coached by Ex-Scotland international full-back, Ken Scotland, while he was Curator at Brodick Castle. Tours have been arranged to England, Wales and Ireland, and the club now run an annual 'sevens' tournament on the island in which teams from many parts of the country participate. Apart from a small grant obtained through the S.R.U., the club is financed by local fund raising and by participants paying their own expenses.

ARRAN LADIES' HOCKEY CLUB was formed in 1989. Players are drawn from all parts of the island and from a wide variety of occupations and age groups. The team competes in Division IV of the West District Hockey Leagues, having been promoted from Divisions VI and V in the first two years of their participation. Except for some sponsorship, the club is financed by local fund raising and by players and officials paying their own expenses. Home matches are played at Arran High School.

PRIZE LIST.

—◦◦◦——

GAMES.—Starting at 1 p.m.

	First.	Second.	Third.
1. Throwing the Hammer, ...	10s	5s	—
2. Putting the Ball, ...	10s	5s	—
3. Flat Race, 100 Yards, Boys under 12 years of age, ...	5s	2s 6d	1s
4. Flat Race, 100 Yards, ...	10s	5s	2s 6d
5. Flat Race, 150 Yards, Boys under 15 years of age, ...	7s 6d	5s	2s 6d
6. Flat Race, Girls under 12 years, ...	5s	4s	2s 6d
7. Flat Race, 300 Yards, ...	10s	7s 6d	5s
8. Long Leap, ...	10s	5s	—
9. High Leap, ...	10s	5s	—
10. Hop, Step, and Leap, ...	10s	5s	—
11. Half-Mile Race, ...	20s	10s	—
12. Tug-of-War (Standing) 6 Men a-side, ...	30s	20s	—
13. Hurdle Race, ...	10s	5s	—
14. Sack Race (over Hurdles),...	7s 6d	5s	—

HORSE RACES.

	First.	Second.	Third.
15. Trotting Match for Ponies, 13 hands and under	30s	20s	10s
16. Handicap Trotting Match, ...	40s	20s	—

INDUSTRIAL EXHIBITION will be held in a Marquee on the Field.

1. For the best Plaid, any Pattern, Hand Spun, Dyed, Waulked, and Woven in Arran—1st, 10s ; 2nd, 5s ; 3rd, 2s 6d.

2. For the best Web of Gentlemen's Cloth, any Pattern, Hand Spun, Dyed, Waulked, and Woven in Arran—1st 10s ; 2nd, 5s ; 3rd, 2s 6d.
   Prizes in above Two Classes offered by Mrs J. P. B. Robertson.

3. For best Web of Ladies' Cloth, any Pattern, Hand Spun, Dyed, Dressed and Woven in Arran—1st, 10s ; 2nd, 5s ; 3rd, 2s 6d.
   In Nos 2 and 3 the Webs must be not less than a Suit or Dress Length, and must be Rolled or Folded full width.

4. For best Web of Drugget, Dyed and Manufactured in Arran—1st, 10s ; 2nd, 5s ; 3rd, 2s 6d. The Exhibit must be of one Pattern, and contain not less than 3 yards.
   Prizes in above Two Classes offered by Mrs A. Graham Murray.

INDUSTRIAL EXHIBITION (Continued.)

5. For the best Pair of Diced Hose, Knitted in Arran, of any Yarn, by Exhibitor—1st, 10s ; 2nd, 5s ; 3rd, 2s 6d.

6. For the best Pair of Rough Kilt Hose, Knitted in Arran, of Home Spun Yarn, by Exhibitor—1st, 7s 6d ; 2nd, 5s ; 3rd, 2s 6d.

   For the best Specimen of Ladies' White Night Dress made in Arran by Exhibitor. The sewing must be done entirely by hand, and any Trimming must also be hand sewed or knitted, and the Exhibit must not be washed or dressed.—1st, £1 ; 2nd 12s 6d ; 3rd, 7s 6d.
   Prizes offered by Her Grace the Duchess of Hamilton.

8. For best Specimen of White Embroidery executed in Arran by Exhibitor.—1st, 10s : 2nd, 5s ; 3rd, 2s 6d.

9. For the best Specimen of Art Needlework, executed in Arran by Exhibitor.—1st, 10s ; 2nd, 5s ; 3rd, 2s 6d.

10. For the best Fancy Shawl of any Pattern, knitted in Arran by Exhibitor.—1st 10s ; 2nd, 5s ; 3rd, 2s 6d.

11. For the best Piece of Relief Wood Carving.—1st 10s; 2nd, 5s; 3rd, 2s 6d.

12. For the best Piece of Surface Wood Carving.—1st, 10s ; 2nd, 5s ; 3rd, 2s 6d.

13. For the best Piece of Chip Carving. —1st, 10s ; 2nd, 5s ; 3rd, 2s 6d.

14. —For the best Model of a Ship, House, Machine, Implement, or any Engineering Work.—1st, 10s ; 2nd, 5s ; 3rd, 2s 6d.

NOTE. —Neither Crochet nor Arasene Work allowed.

All Competitions are strictly Confined to Residents in Arran. No 3rd Prize will be given unless Four compete, nor a 2nd if only Two.

Competitors must be ready within Five Minutes after the announcement of each event or be disqualified.

Entries for Horse Races Nos. 15 and 16, must be lodged with the Secretary on or before FRIDAY, 19th curt , and no Horse may be Entered which has not been the *bona-fide* property of the Entrant for at least One Month previous.

INDUSTRIAL EXHIBITION.—All Articles must be delivered to the Secretary before Eight o'clock p.m on FRIDAY, 19th curt, and cannot be received later.

This Programme is subject to any alteration the Committee may think proper. In all disputes the Committee's decision shall be final.

Admission to the Field and Exhibition, - - - Sixpence;

A BAND WILL BE IN ATTENDANCE DURING THE DAY.

R. HAMILTON, Secretary.

Brodick Highland Games & Exhibition of Native Industrial Work
Saturday 20th August, 1898

BRODICK HIGHLAND GAMES have been held in August of each year since 1886, except for the duration of each world war and short breaks at the beginning of the century and early in the 1960's. Gate receipts in 1886 were £13 3/6d and it is estimated that about 500 people attended. Track and field events were much the same as at present but for several years competitors were confined to residents of Arran. In 1890, the scope of the Games was widened to include a regatta and 'a competitive exhibition of native industrial work', classes for the latter including cloth woven, dyed and waulked on the island; knitting; needlework; wood carving; and model making. Many famous athletes have competed in the sports, including several who have taken part in the Olympic Games. Throughout their history, the Games have been well supported and sponsored by the local Ducal family and in the 1950's the prizes were presented by Prince Ranier of Monaco while he was on holiday at Brodick Castle. In 1979, the world famous Pipes and Drums of the Scots Guards attracted a record crowd of 3,200.

BRODICK REGATTA in the 1890's — held as part of Brodick Highland Games.

THE GOATFELL RACE Challenge Cup was inaugurated in 1953 and, except for a few brief breaks, has been run annually since then. The race starts and finishes in Ormidale Park in the centre of Brodick and attracts good class runners from all over the U.K. A new record time of 1 hour 13 minutes and 11 seconds was set in 1992, breaking the existing record by 2 seconds. The first female to compete was a 16 years old Brodick girl, Betty Corbett, who ran the course barefooted in 1956. The race is now organised by Arran Runners who took over from the island's tourist board a few years ago. The photograph shows Arran's Tourist Officer, Charles Currie, facing the camera, setting an example by competing in the event.

The Man from Toronto.

A Comedy in Three Acts by Douglas Murray

CAST :

Mrs CALTHORPE (a young widow), -	Mlle de LARABRIE
FERGUS WIMBUSH { (a Canadian over on his } first visit to England) }	Mr A. K. WOOLEY
RUTH WIMBUSH (his elder Sister), - - -	LADY GRAHAM
ADA WIMBUSH (his younger sister), - -	Miss E. SWEET
ROBT. GILMOUR { (Mrs Calthorpe's young } cousin on a visit to } Beach House)	Mr A. MONTGOMERY
Mr PRIESTLY (Guardian, etc., to Mrs Calthorpe),	LORD GRAHAM
MARTHA (Parlourmaid), - -	Miss ELLALINE SILLARS
Mrs HUBBARD, - - -	The DUCHESS of HAMILTON
MINNIE HUBBARD (her daughter),-	LADY MARY GRAHAM

ARRAN DRAMATIC SOCIETY There is no surprise in knowing that in 1920, Arran Dramatic Society performed the 3-Act comedy 'The Man From Toronto' in Lamlash Public Hall and that 500 people attended. Nevertheless, many people will be surprised to see that the cast list includes The Duchess of Hamilton, Lord and Lady Graham (the future Duke and Duchess of Montrose), and Lady Mary Graham. In the following year, members of the cast, except for The Duchess of Hamilton, and supplemented by local actors, Mrs. Stewart Orr, Mr. T. Walker and Mr. C. Currie, performed a 3-Act farce 'Eliza Comes To Stay' for two nights in the same hall.

SHEEP DOG TRIALS on the island are popular with residents and visitors alike. The standard is high with well known mainland handlers and their dogs competing against strong local opposition. Dougarie trials, held on Machrie golf course, began in 1888, and are the third oldest trials in Scotland. Kildonan and District Sheepdog Association, which was formed in 1970, hold their trials on the Home Farm, Brodick. The photograph is of the judges at Dougarie trials soon after their inauguration.

BRODICK GOLF CLUB.
NEW COURSE.

The above COURSE will be OPENED

ON

Saturday First, 10th July, 1897,

AT FOUR O'CLOCK, P.M.,

BY

ROBERT M'LELLAND, Esq.

ADMISSION (ON OPENING DAY),   -   - FREE.

PRINTED BY A. GUTHRIE & SONS, ARDROSSAN

This notice referred to a 9-hole course on Mayish Hill, above Invercloy, the first in Brodick, as far as is known.
The existing course opened in 1915.

GOLF is the most popular sport on the island for both locals and visitors. There are seven courses, each an interesting test of skill in a picturesque setting. Lamlash, Brodick and Whiting Bay have 18-hole courses, Shiskine the unusual number of 12 holes, Corrie and Machrie both have 9 holes. In the past there were courses at Kildonan, Pirnmill and Corriecravie. The oldest course is Lamlash which opened in 1892. A feature of most of the courses is an 'honesty box' into which players are trusted to put their fees in the absence of the starter.

Shiskine's first golf clubhouse, pictured around the turn of the century, at which time the course had only 9 holes.

AN ISLAND AT WAR

As the events and effects of two horrific world wars in the first half of this century fade further and further from memory and fewer and fewer of those who were involved are left to reminisce, we become more aware of how quickly we lose the opportunity to record first-hand accounts of history. Unfortunately, knowledge of Arran during the First World War is already scant and prominence has to be given to the Second. Many of the island's young men and women went off and played their parts in war but this is not an account of their experiences, it is about how war affected life on the island.

People who have known Arran only in time of peace may wonder if this beautiful island so far removed from war zones and blitzed cities could have had any appreciable

in Lamlash, with soldiers billeted on families in each village. Amongst the premises taken over by the army were Lochranza Youth Hostel; Whitehouse, Lamlash; and Douglas Hotel, Brodick; the last-named being the Combined Operations H.Q. for the island.

Day after day and night after night, the Commandos marched, ran and scrambled over the roads and hills of Arran. They scaled the peaks, waded the rivers, and swam fully-kitted in the sea, until they were thoroughly toughened, trained and disciplined. Brave young men who distinguished themselves in various theatres of war were honed to perfection on Arran. Between them they won many awards for bravery, including a Victoria Cross awarded to Lieutenant Geoffrey Keyes who had been

Eighty horses requisitioned from Arran farms going off to the First World War, on P.S. Duchess of Hamilton in 1914.

involvement in war.

The people of the island were used to having regular visits from naval ships and to hosting Royal Navy personnel. Lamlash had been a busy naval base during the 1914/18 war and a popular anchorage for the navy between the wars, and in 1939 it was anticipated that the island would become an important wartime base once more. Nevertheless, it was with the military that the island was involved first in the Second World War. Arran was to be a battle training ground for the army's daring Commando units and the first of them were shipped to the island in 1940. No.7 Commando were stationed in Lochranza, No.9 Commando in Whiting Bay, and No.11 Commando

well known in Lamlash as the local billeting officer. Later in the war, a few thousand Canadian troops came to the island for their final pre-invasion training before they went off to take part in the hazardous landing on Sicily.

Throughout the war, Lamlash was a bustling naval base with seldom less than ten warships at anchor in the bay, protected by an anti-submarine net which extended from Clauchlands Point to Holy Isle, and a series of similar nets which formed a zig-zag passage between Kingcross and Holy Isle. The village was also a naval gunnery station and daily, wooden targets which had been made or repaired in what is now the Sailing club shed, were towed out into the Firth and blasted by ships' guns. The dull thud of the guns was a regular background noise along most of the east and south coasts of the island.

In Lamlash, Marine House was the Naval Base H.Q. and Harport the Boom Defence Office; High Trees was the Naval Sick Bay with its cottage as the Dental Surgery; Kinneil and Altachorvie were W.R.N.S. quarters and Arran High School was a naval barracks with up to 200 accommodated at any one time; Officers lived in Whitehouse, and Point House, Kingscross was the Naval Signals Office. Brodick, Whiting Bay and Lochranza were visited regularly by naval ships and, as Lamlash was also a landing craft training station, the crews of these vessels held mock-invasions on many of the island's beaches.

In 1943, many Arran people witnessed one of the worst inshore naval disasters of the war when H.M.S. Dasher, a small aircraft carrier, exploded and sank quickly about four miles off Merkland Point. According to the

young airmen met Death on its mountains, and many local men witnessed scenes and took part in work they never thought to experience.

The first air crash of the war was in February, 1941, when an Anson aircraft flew into the side of Am Binnein, above High Corrie, with the loss of five men. In August of the same year, twenty-two men died when a Liberator en route from Prestwick to the U.S.A., returning air crew who had ferried planes across the Atlantic, crashed near Coire Nam Fuaran, a half mile east of the first crash. In daylight in August, 1942, in full view of hundreds of people in Brodick, a Beaufort flew into the side of Goatfell, and three men perished. In the same month, another Anson crashed north of Lochranza and five men were killed. Four weeks later, an Albecore of the Fleet Air Arm crashed late at night near Shiskine, followed shortly by the daylight crash of a Seafire fighter near Aucheleffan, north of Kilmory; the fates of the crews of these aircraft

Men of the 11th commando visiting the Isle of Arran Heritage Museum during their re-union in 1985

official enquiry, 379 men lost their lives and 149 were rescued, many of whom were badly burned. The vessel had left its anchorage in Lamlash Bay shortly before the accident. The cause of the explosion was not ascertained but was probably due to a fault in the carrier's aviation fuel system.

Almost every evening throughout the war years, hundreds of servicemen were off duty in the villages of Arran and social life has never been so active. Many local girls married soldiers or sailors and several of the men returned and settled on the island. The men of 11th Commando have retained their connection with Arran and still hold an annual re-union on the island.

Arran's connection with the airmen of the Second World War was one of death and destruction. No. R.A.F. personnel were stationed on the island but over fifty

is not known. Two girls trudging up Glen Catacol in 1943 found the wreckage of a Chesapeake with its crew dead. The last two crashes of the war were both on Ben Nuis; first, a Liberator flying into Prestwick from the U.S.A. came to grief with the loss of ten men, and then a Lodestar which had taken off from Prestwick hit the mountain and killed eight men.

The locations of the worst of the crashes were scenes of carnage and destruction which teams of police, doctors and local men had to reach and deal with in all weathers and at all times of day. The stables at Brodick Castle were used as a mortuary and estate workers and local shepherds gave invaluable service as guides. The bodies of most of the young men have been returned for burial near their homes but twenty-one still lie in the peace of Kilbride Cemetery, Lamlash.

The graves of 21 wartime air crash victims in Kilbride Cemetery, Lamlash

On Arran, as in every city, town and village in the U.K., people gave liberally of their time during the Second World War, serving in one or other of the civilian defence organisations. Women played a major part; some drove ambulances, the Women's Land Army worked hard on farms in place of men who had gone off to the forces, and the ladies of the W.V.S, while caring for and counselling young men and women of the services on the island, also turned out with a 'chuck wagon' to give support and sustenance to men engaged in major incidents.

Although the army and navy had their own medical services on the island, the local doctors and the hospital were stretched to their limits. Patient lists doubled or trebled overnight. In addition to the normal birthrate, almost one hundred 'service babies' were born in the hospital in four years (service baby is not defined in the statistics). Bodies were washed ashore from ships lost at sea and, as had to be done for every air crash victim, they had to be examined and identified.

Before the war, a police sergeant and two constables had operated in a peaceful island community in which they knew everyone and there was no crime of consequence. During the war they had to cope with several thousands of taut-nerved young men from every part of Britain and abroad. They had to attend and report on every air crash, supervising the retrieval and identification of the victims. A few of their many other wartime duties were the billeting of servicemen and evacuees, the circulation of particulars of army and navy absentees to other police forces, and enquiries regarding supposed spies around the island. For assistance, they had only one War Reserve Constable, and several excellent Special Constables around the island.

Early in the war, an influx of evacuees from Glasgow and Greenock caused their own special problems. Every part of the island accommodated its share and the small island schools had difficulty in coping with the increased numbers of children, an example of which is noted in the book 'History of the Villages of the Isle of Arran', published by the ladies of the Arran S.W.R.I. Corrie School saw its roll rise from 45 to 200 almost overnight and had to close for ten days to re-organise; when it opened again it did so with two local and two evacuee teachers operating a shift system for children. Many of the evacuated families could not cope with island life and drifted back to their homes; other families stayed on permanently and some are still on the island.

Although this is an account of life on the island during wartime, it would be wrong not to acknowledge the young men of Arran who made the supreme sacrifice, losing their lives in the service of their country. In total, 89 died in the First World War and 40 in the Second, a heavy toll for a small community.

As a consequence of the First World War, Arran got its first proper general hospital. There had been isolation hospitals, first at Lamlash and later at Whiting Bay, but no other hospital facility. In 1919, when meetings were being held to organise fund-raising for the erection of war memorials, the Marchioness of Graham suggested that a suitable form of remembrance would be a cottage hospital. The suggestion was supported unanimously and the site at Lamlash was gifted by Arran Estate. Money was raised throughout the island and the Isle of Arran War Memorial Hospital accepted its first patients in May, 1922.

Left:- Catherine Kerr, Blackwaterfoot, in Land Army uniform.

Right:- Betty Campbell, Shiskine, in a Land Girl's normal working gear. A local girl, she was the island's first Land Girl.

THE WOMEN'S LAND ARMY was well represented on Arran during the Second World War. When the conflict started, young women could choose to join the services, work in munitions factories or join the Land Army. Although most farm workers were exempt from conscription to the services, the need for greatly increased food production required many more people on the land. Young women from all walks of life many of whom had never been near a farm or animals, joined the Land Army and served for the duration of the war. They made a great contribution of the country's war effort and can look back with pride in their work and amusement at their experiences. Several married into the local farming community.

Fifty years on, seven ex-Land Army girls live on the island. Pictured below with Grace Small, President of the Heritage Museum (back row, second left) are:- Catherine Kerr, Martha Currie, Peggy Currie, Millie Logan and Betty Campbell. Not present are Annie Stewart and Margaret Davidson.

The Marchioness of Graham (later Duchess of Montrose)
laying the foundation stone of the Isle of Arran War Memorial Hospital in 1921

THE VILLAGES

BRODICK. This photograph illustrates the early development of the modern village. The village hall, opened in 1895, is seen on the left behind Auchenard. The large building in the centre foreground was Adolph Ribbeck's shop and is now the Co-op Store. The Chemist's shop was built in 1886 as the post office. The bowling green and tennis courts were not opened until 1908 and 1918 respectively. The water beside the hall may have been the pond known as the 'Puddocky'.

This view of ROSABURN, BRODICK from outside The Primary School dates from around the time of the First World War. The standing stone is as we know it at present and the building on the left is now part of the Isle of Arran Heritage Museum. Since the picture was taken, houses have been built all along the far side of the road. The rough, unsurfaced condition of the road is a reminder that most of Arran's roads were not surfaced with tar until the 1920's. Although it is not in the picture, the school had been built in 1854.

INVERCLOY VILLAGE, BRODICK

When this view was published in a book of photographs called 'Picturesque Arran' early in the 1920's, it was accompanied by the caption - 'There is no actual village of Brodick, which really consists of the pier and a few scattered houses. Invercloy is some little distance from the pier.' The caption indicates that it took much longer than is realised generally for the composite parts of the modern village to forego their separate identities. The large house nearest the camera is Tigh Na Mara. Some of the low white cottages in the picture still exist.

Until the 1920's LAMLASH SMIDDY stood on the corner site in the centre of the village now occupied by Aldersyde Hotel and its public bar. When the buildings were demolished the blacksmith moved his workshop to a site on the west side of Whiting Bay Road, beyond Arranton Bridge.

The thatched cottages of NICOL STREET, Lamlash, stood along the west side of the back road, south of Claveron Road. The date 1899 , on the house Dalgoram, on the site, shows that the cottages were demolished before then.

SHORE ROAD, LAMLASH. Until the 1930's, Sillars Hotel (now Glenisle) on the left, was a centre of social life in the village as it had a large room on the ground floor in which the Girl Guides, Brownies, a dancing class and various other organisations held their meetings. The cottage attached to the far end of the hotel was the police station until the present office was opened in the 1930's. Beyond the station is Lilybank, the far end of which was Kerr's butcher's shop from 1924 to 1974. Next in line is Undercliffe, home and surgery of Doctor James Buchanan, General Practitioner in the village and Surgeon in the hospital for over 30 years.

Paddle steamer 'Juno' off KINGSCROSS JETTY in the early years of this century. The smoke from its funnel suggests that it is about to get underway now that the small ferry is well clear. Although there was never a pier, steamers called regularly until the 1930's. The driver of the horse and cart may have driven into the sea to soak the wooden wheels, the joints of which tended to loosen in hot weather.

KINGSCROSS POST OFFICE in the 1920's. On the right is a G.M.C. omnibus owned by Ernest Bolt of Lamlash which was operated on a fairly frequent service connecting Brodick, Lamlash, Kingscross, and Whiting Bay. On the left is McNeish's horse-drawn van from Lamlash with its driver, Geordie Moore, and the post office assistant, Maggie Smith. The post office, now part of the house 'Birchdene', was closed in the 1970's on the death of Alan Cook who had been postmaster for almost sixty years.

KINGSCROSS POINT has several interesting historical associations, the oldest being the remains of an iron age fort dating from between two and three thousand years ago. The circular fort is about thirty-five feet in diameter, enclosed by a wall which has been reduced to about three feet in height but is up to twelve feet thick in places. A few feet west of the fort are the remains of a Viking boat burial, dating from the 9th century. Amongst the articles which have been excavated from the grave are a ship's rivets and nails, an engraved piece of bone and a Viking coin dating from 854 A.D. The area takes its name from its legendary association with Robert Bruce, King Robert I of Scotland. Tradition maintains that in 1307, with his band of followers in thirty small boats, Bruce crossed from the Point to Turnberry on the Ayrshire coast to start the campaign that led to his victory at Bannockburn and to England's recognition of Scotland as a separate nation. A man called Cuthbert had been sent on ahead to spy out the land and, if circumstances were favourable, to light a fire on the hillside above Turnberry as a signal for Bruce and his men to follow. Cuthbert found conditions in Ayrshire to be far from propitious and decided against lighting the signal, however, some other hand lit a fire and Bruce set out on the campaign that might have been postponed or have taken Scottish history along another course. A few yards below the level of the ancient fort, the remains of a Second World War gun emplacement is a reminder that mankind has learned so little about living in peace with their neighbours.

S.S. Duchess of Hamilton leaving WHITING BAY PIER. Of all photographs of the pierhead, this is probably the earliest, having been taken soon after the pier opened in 1901. Cattle are seen grazing in the area that is now the car park. The building on the extreme right housed the pier office and waiting room and is now part of the Old Pier Shop.

A view from WHITING BAY PIER shortly before the First World War. The house directly opposite the pierhead was the village police station until late in the 1970's and the semi-detached thatched cottage on the left of the station is now the two-storied house 'Thornvale'. Behind the tree on the right of the pierhead there was a row of thatched cottages which were not demolished until the 1930's. The properties which are Kiscadale Hotel and 'The Pantry' restaurant are prominent in the picture.

The south end of WHITING BAY early in the 1900's . The house nearest the camera was Cooper Angus, which has been demolished and its grounds developed as a holiday park. Behind it is Pleasantfield, with its stacks and stooks showing it to have been a croft. The next large house is now the Youth Hostel, behind which the houses Tigh-an-Uillt, Ardow, Silverbank Cottage, Stanford and The Riggs can be seen.

KILDONAN has never had a man-made harbour or pier but the small sheltered bay called the Yellow Port was a regular port of call for sailing smacks and puffers transporting freight to and from the south-east corner of Arran. Vessels sailed in and out at high tide, and transferred their cargoes when high and dry at low tide.

KILDONAN HOTEL AND PLADDA, photographed about 1910. The disused lifeboat shed is in the centre, close to the sea. The small hay ricks in the field in the foreground illustrate part of the method of harvesting the crop in use until recent years. Ricks were of a convenient size for transporting to the farm for storage. Pladda island and lighthouse are in the background. The island was the site of an ancient chapel dedicated to St. Blaise.

KILDONAN LIFEBOAT attended its last call-out in January, 1908, and the photograph was probably taken shortly before that date. It is not clear whether the crowd has attended to watch a real or practice launching. The lifeboat had no engine and had to be rowed to emergencies, mostly in adverse weather conditions. It was withdrawn due to lack of demand for its services and replaced with a crew of Auxiliary Coastguards equipped with rescue apparatus.

HIGH CLOINED which was about one and a half miles north-east of KILMORY. The ruins of the cottages are now in the midst of a forest of conifers. Although the cottages look primitive, glass paned windows have replaced the wooden shutters which would close the window spaces originally. The peat stack is a reminder of the difficulty our forebears had in obtaining fuel . Even if the source of the peat was close to home, it took a man working alone for ten or twelve hours per day, a month to cut, dry, transport and stack enough peat to last his family through a winter, even though the fuel was used mainly for cooking rather than for heating. Whereas peat was free and coal had to be bought, if coal could be afforded it saved a great deal of hard, time-consuming labour.

SLIDDERY SCHOOL AND SCHOOLHOUSE, photographed in 1909. Built in 1860, the school drew pupils from Sliddery, Corriecave and Bennecarrigan until it closed in 1946, since when primary pupils have been transported to Kilmory School and secondary pupils to Arran High School, Lamlash. The buildings, which have also housed a shop and post office, are still in existence.

SLIDDERY'S OLD SHOP no longer exists. It sat back from the north side of the main road, immediately east of the house 'Bon Vista', on the site now occupied by a large barn. When photographed in the 1930's, the shop was owned by Sandy McKelvie who also operated the grocery van seen on the left of the picture. The van in the centre was owned by James McKelvie, butcher, Whiting Bay, who was not related to Sandy.

CORRIECRAVIE GOLF CLUB MEMBERS outside their clubhouse on the opening of their new nine-hole course on The Corries. Earlier, there had been a course on Corriecravie Farm. The new course closed on the outbreak of the Second World War. Until recent years, Corriecravie and Sliddery each had tennis courts and several boarding houses, as well as sharing a school, a smiddy, a joiner, a draper, a shoemaker and a garage, of which only the garage still operates, a loss of local amenities common to all rural areas of the island.

BLACKWATERFOOT did not exist as a village until the last quarter of the 19th century. Until then there were only a few scattered houses, an inn and a small farm. The mouth of the Black Water was the harbour for Shiskine and the surrounding area and the tenantry contributed towards the cost of a small ferry which connected them with Campbeltown. Around the 1880's, the location began to attract development and soon its beautiful bay and sandy beach became popular with tourists. Various amenities followed, including the golf course which opened in 1896.

HAMILTON ARMS, SHISKINE, now Arran Outdoor Centre, is the two-storey building near the centre of this late 19th century photograph. As a hotel, it was one of Arran's most popular for about a hundred years. In 1981, its owner, Miss Mary Currie, gave it over to The Abernethy Trust who run it as a Christian holiday centre offering a range of outdoor activities for adults and children. The centre also accommodates up to 40 primary school children on short environmental and nature study courses.

SHISKINE VILLAGE, looking towards Shedog, photographed in the 1890's.

MACHRIE POST OFFICE & SHOP, with the mail cum passenger coach on the coast road, early in the 1900's. The property 'Dunedin', still owned by the Weir family, was operated by them as the post office until about the time of the Second World War.

DOUGARIE LODGE was built as a sporting lodge by the 11th Duke of Hamilton. In the middle of the 19th century, when Queen Victoria set a fashion of shooting and fishing holidays in Scotland, most of the country's landowners developed their estates so that they could entertain their friends. The 11th Duke had the north end of Arran developed as a deer forest and most of the high ground as grouse muirs. Dougarie and Dippen Lodges were built to accommodate his sporting guests. Both are now privately owned. Dougarie Lodge is beautifully situated at the mouth of Glen Iorsa on the west coast of the island. Until several years ago, the outside walls were decorated with antlers and was a source of interest for visitors to the island. In 1891, Arran's first telephone was installed between Brodick Castle and Dougarie Lodge.

PIRNMILL, viewed from the sea, in the 1880's. The tall building on the right is the 'pirn' (bobbin) mill which operated from 1780 to 1840 and from which the village took its modern name. The mill building is now a private dwelling-house. Other properties in the picture are the village store, boarding house, post office and smiddy.

PIRNMILL VILLAGE STORE AND BOARDING HOUSE, photographed late in the 19th century. A second storey has been added to the middle property, which is now The Anvil Tearoom.

PIRNMILL GOLF COURSE was immediately above the village, between the Mill Burn and the school. A 9-hole course, it opened in the 1890's and closed on the outbreak of the Second World War when the land was taken over for agricultural purposes. The clubhouse is still extant as a farm outbuilding.

CATACOL FARM was built as a hunting lodge early in the 1840's by Henry Westenha, later Lord Rossmore, an Irish Baron related to the Duke of Hamilton by marriage. His wife had inherited a parcel of land in the area and he intended to create a small shooting estate. Twelve families were cleared out of Glen Catacol to make way for deer. The row of small cottages called THE TWELVE APOSTLES were built near the shore at the mouth of the glen but the families refused to occupy them, many preferring to move away, and they stood empty for about two years. As the land reverted to the Hamilton family in 1845, it is not clear which landowner built the cottages.

LOCHRANZA BARKING HOUSE, which stands between the main road and the Ranza Burn, at the east end of the village, was built by the Millers of Knockenrioch who owned several large fishing vessels. In the building, the local fishing fleet's nets were steeped in vats of an astringent liquor called cutch, catechu or cashoo which was obtained by boiling tree bark imported from India or Burma and was regarded as the best preservative available. After they had been soaked, the nets were hung out to dry on frames which stood on the green in front of the building. Every fishing fleet harbour had a barking house; the ruins of another can be traced at Pirnmill.

The S.S. Kintyre at LOCHRANZA PIER around 1890. Reckoned to have been one of the most beautiful steamers to have sailed on the Clyde, the vessel was on the Glasgow/Lochranza/Pirnmill/Campbeltown service for thirty-nine years. She was sunk in a collision with another ship off Wemyss Bay in 1907. The pier went out of use in 1957, fell into a dangerous state of disrepair, and was finally swept away in a storm in 1989.

CORRIE HARBOUR and the trading smack Glen Sannox in the 1890's. Owned by Kelso of Corrie, the 40 feet smack was built at Ardrossan in 1878 and traded out of Arran villages until the 1920's.

FERRY ROCK, CORRIE and the P.S. Ivanhoe in the 1890's. Although the village never had a pier at which steamers could berth, the vessels called regularly until the 1930's. As passengers had to be transferred by a small ferry boat, the elderly and very young generally travelled via Brodick.

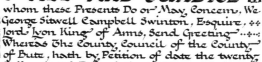

TO·ALL·AND·SUNDRY whom these Presents Do or May Concern, We George Sitwell Campbell Swinton, Esquire, Lord Lyon King of Arms, Send Greeting: Whereas The County Council of the County of Bute, hath by Petition of date the twenty first day of May last, Prayed that We would Grant Our Licence and Authority unto them and to the County of Bute to bear and use such Ensigns Armorial as might be found suitable and according to the laws of Arms, Know ye therefore that We have Devised and Do by these Presents Assign, Ratify, and Confirm unto the Petitioners The County Council of the County of Bute and to the said County, the following Ensigns Armorial as depicted upon the margin hereof and matriculated of even date with these Presents in Our Public Register of All Arms and Bearings in Scotland viz:— Parted per pale, on the dexter, Parted per fess Gules and Argent, in chief three cinquefoils two and one Ermine, and in base a lymphad, sails furled Sable, flagged of the first, and in the sinister Or, a fess chequy Azure and Argent. In Testimony whereof these Presents are subscribed by Us and the Seal of Our Office is affixed hereunto at Edinburgh on the eighth day of July in the eighteenth year of the Reign of Our Sovereign Lord, George the Fifth by the Grace of God of Great Britain, Ireland and of the British Dominions beyond the Seas, King, Defender of the Faith, Emperor of India, &c. and in the year of Our Lord One thousand nine hundred & twenty seven

Lyon.

From ancient times, Arran was associated closely with the Isle of Bute and as early as 1452 was referred to as being in that island's Sheriffdom. In 1885, as part of the County of Bute, Arran began to be administered partly from Rothesay and from 1929 it elected six members to Bute County Council, in addition to having its own District Council.

Since 1975, the island has been part of Cunninghame District of Strathclyde Region.